For Michael J. Crew
With all good wishes

Norman Nowells
Nov '84

FAREWELL THE ISLANDS

by

ROSCOE HOWELLS

Gomer Press
1987

First Impression - October 1987

ISBN 0 86383 328 4

Printed by Gomer Press, Llandysul, Dyfed

For
the many friends who have
afforded me the pleasure of
introducing them to
The Islands.

Acknowledgements

There has been no great amount of research involved in the writing of this book, so those whose help has had to be enlisted are not as numerous as usual. Even so, the help which has been necessary is none the less important.

It will be evident that I have reason to be particularly grateful to Mrs. Margaret Davies for making available the fascinating letters and other documents relating to Capt Vaughan Palmer Davies.

At the Pembrokeshire Records Office, the County Archivist, Mr. Clive Hughes, and his Assistant, Mrs. Coreen Streets, were always prepared to go to endless trouble on my behalf as was, as usual, Mrs. Joan Evans at the County Library. I am also grateful to Mr. David Saunders for letting me see the old minutes of the West Wales Field Society.

It was not easy to find pictures which I have not used in previous books and I am, therefore, grateful to all those who have helped to provide pictures which may not have appeared before.

A considerable part of this book consists of reproducing passages, both of my own work and of others, which have previously appeared elsewhere. All these sources are acknowledged in their appropriate places and I would here thank those who have readily given permission for their use in these pages.

Over the years I have been grateful to the many boatmen and others who have made it possible for me to visit the islands so extensively and I acknowledge that indebtedness.

Once again I have to thank my wife for so much support in typing, proof-reading, tedious indexing and the many suggestions which go towards the making of a book. Without that help the book would have been much the poorer.

Finally, a warm thank-you to Ian Niall, whose own writing I admire so much, not only for his ready agreement when asked to write the Foreword, but for his more than generous references.

R.H.

Contents

Foreword

Roscoe Howells is one of a rare breed of men who are deeply interested in social history and happen to be blessed with a gift that enables them to communicate what they have discovered. Quite unsentimental in his approach, as one would expect of a man with a farming background, Roscoe has a deep love of those timeless, off-shore islands that have inspired his earlier works. One reads his accounts on the life on the sun-blessed, summer islands and can hear the yelping gulls, the endless hushing of the sea, and feel the warmth radiating from the fine, rabbit-trimmed turf. Sheep bleat and seabirds sail and dive, and nothing disturbs the even tenor of the day for the people Roscoe writes about. He has researched his subject thoroughly on every occasion, and he has unearthed human documents that give his writing a wonderful authority. I have known him for thirty years and have never ceased to be impressed by him. He is a believer, a very sincere man, and *The Sounds Between*, following *Cliffs of Freedom*, both of which are before me as I write, established him as the rightful historian of Skomer, Ramsey, Skokholm and Grassholm. He went on to write of Caldey later. *Farewell the Islands* may be said to complete his saga of a world far from the madding crowd, but it will not, I trust, be his last work. He is a forthright man who has strong opinions. It would be a pity if he didn't employ his talent on some equally rewarding aspect of life in his beloved country.

Ian Niall, Five Acres,
Ashley Green, Bucks.

Introduction

It is more than twenty-five years since my book, *Cliffs of Freedom*, dealing mainly with Reuben Codd of Skomer, was published, and almost twenty years since *The Sounds Between*, which dealt with Skomer, Ramsey, Skokholm and Grassholm, whilst the second edition had a section on Caldey as well.

My two books dealing specifically with Caldey were published much more recently, yet, even in that short time, various bits of information have since come to light and I found myself wondering whether I ought to put together another book to bring the story, as far as I know it, up-to-date.

When I wrote *Cliffs of Freedom* I said that many people must have lived on the islands over the years whose stories would have made some marvellous books and yet, because no one had made a record of such people, their stories were lost for ever. By the time I came to research in much more detail, and wrote *The Sounds Between*, the truth of this assertion had become abundantly clear, and of nobody could it have been more clearly true than of Vaughan Palmer Davies, who farmed on Skomer for thirty years in the second half of the 19th century.

Of him, I had written so much that it never occurred to me that he or his family would figure prominently in any sort of miscellany such as I had in mind. Then, in the autumn of 1984, I had a letter from a lady in London, a Mrs. Margaret Davies, to say that her husband had died, at the age of eighty-nine. She was having to move house and had many papers of which to dispose, including papers of her husband's family and, as I had shown an interest in that family in the past, could I ensure their safe-keeping. Her husband's name was Vaughan Palmer Davies, and he had been a grandson of the one of that name who had farmed Skomer from 1861 to 1892.

Those papers are now safely stored in the Pembrokeshire Records Office in Haverfordwest, and what a wealth of material is in them. So many of them are letters written to the young

Captain Vaughan Palmer Davies when he was at sea in the Far East and are outside the scope of any such work as this. But they do shed great light on many aspects of life in Pembrokeshire at the time and will be a valuable source of reference for students. More than one book could be written about them. The courtship of young Ellen Robinson of Skomer, whom Captain Davies eventually married, would make a full length romance in itself.

Apart from any idea of bringing the story up-to-date for the sake of the record for posterity, there have also been odd items which I have written occassionally for less well-known publications, and the thought occurred that they could be of some small interest to those who know the islands, enjoy reading about them, and would probably have missed such items when they appeared. Would there, I wondered, be enough of such material to warrant another book. Then I came across all those letters, and already I realise that the question now will be how much I shall have to leave out.

My hope is that, together, they will make a book which will be acceptable to the many who have so far received kindly what I have written of the islands of my native county.

Chapter 1

Letters From Home

Captain Vaughan Palmer Davies took over on Skomer in 1861 and left there in March 1892. An entry in the 'writing album', which had been given to his wife by grateful visitors a few years previously, was made by their daughter Claire who had been born there and was still living with them. It read, 'Mr Vaughan Davies and family left 'Skomer Island' in March 1892 to reside at 'The Mumbles' near Swansea. It was with many regrets that they had to say 'Farewell Isle of Birds and Beauty'.'

Although it is known, from pictures and other sources, that the sea-birds were there in their countless thousands in those days, and that their eggs were taken, there is surprisingly little reference to them in any of the letters. There is much more reference to birds that were shot, including the senseless shooting of the puffins, and to birds that were stuffed and put into glass cases.

Vaughan Davies's great-great-grandmother was Hannah Vaughan, one of David Garrick's three principal leading ladies, so that explains the Christian name. Palmer was his mother's maiden name.

He was one of the twelve children of Thomas Mathias Davies and his wife, Emily Alicia, who farmed at Broom Hill near Dale. There were eight boys and four girls. A boy and a girl died in infancy, one boy was drowned at Calcutta at the age of twenty-six, and the remainder lived to a ripe old age.

Two of the girls did not marry. Emily, known as 'Bolly', lived to be ninety-three, and Myra, known as 'Pye', lived to be eighty-eight. They were the ones who wrote most of the letters from home, and it is in these letters, as well as in those which Vaughan wrote himself, that there can be seen the great Christian conviction with which they lived their lives. It is known that Vaughan Davies, during his life as skipper of a sailing-clipper, had always conducted morning prayers on board his ship and continued the practice when he lived on Skomer. But this need not have had any great significance in itself. It is the letters which bring to life the real Christian sincerity of the writers.

One of the boys, Henry, became a solicitor, some stayed on the land, and some went to sea. Vaughan became an apprentice aboard the barque 'Worcester' in London in 1844 when he was eighteen years of age. He obtained his mariner's register ticket three years later. This shows that he stood five feet seven-and-a-half inches in height, his hair was light brown and his eyes were grey. He obtained his master's certificate in 1852, when he was still only twenty six, and spent the next decade in the trade between Calcutta, Bombay, Hong-Kong and Singapore. Much of the time he was carrying opium, as was his brother Charles, more often known as 'Carlo'. For the most part his vessels seem to have been the *Poppy* and *The Arrow*.

The Chinese government objected to this activity by British vessels, leading as it did to the degradation of the Chinese people, and two wars resulted from it. The second of the *Opium* wars, in 1857, was started when a ship called the *Arrow*, and flying the British flag, was seized by the 'heathen Chinese'. Although Vaughan was commanding a ship called the *Arrow* at that time there is no knowing whether it was his ship which was involved in the incident.

In 1856 Emily had written to Vaughan and, having expressed some disquietude over the dangers of the trade in which he was involved, went on to say '. . . nor am I *quite* satisfied of the lawfulness of the trade in opium. I don't understand the matter myself but so many of the best people I know think it wrong. . .'

Much of the time Vaughan was known to his family as 'Twany', but sometimes as 'Marmion' and sometimes, to his friends, as 'Jolly Jack'. When writing to his future wife Ellen, or Nelle, Robinson, of Skomer, he sometimes referred to himself as 'Seagull' and to her as 'Puffin'.

When I was researching *The Sounds Between* I was told by the late Mr Edward Scriven, a grandson of Vaughan Davies, that his grandfather had brought one of the old 'coffin ships' home round Cape of Good Hope in a storm, with his wife and their first-born

The Davies girls and Ann Lush blowing guillemots' and razorbills' eggs.

infant son on board. These vessels, often criminally overladen, were likewise heavily over-insured by the owners who hoped never to see them again. Crews were expendable. To their amazement, on this occasion their skipper walked into their offices at Liverpool and the outcome of it was that he told them he wanted nothing more to do with them.

Another grandson, however, the late Mr Percy Valentine Davies, who also gave me tremendous help, assured me that there was nothing at all in this story, and that Vaughan Davies came home from the Far East with the specific intention of taking over on Skomer because of his wife's health. I did not feel, therefore, that I could use the Scriven version of the story, but it is now clear from the letters, and there are many of them, that it was almost certainly true. It is clear that the owner, Forman, was a most undesirable type and a rogue, and that Vaughan had every intention of returning to the sea. Until not long before he eventually took over on Skomer he was still looking for a berth, having qualified in steam. His father-in-law, Edward Robinson, however, finally persuaded him to take over and settle on the island.

Many of the letters were written before ever Vaughan Davies became associated with Skomer and are not, therefore, relevant here, but there are many references to the island because the young people were friendly with Edward Robinson's two daughters and son, Tom. What eventually became of Tom I do not know, but there is much which shows the subterfuge that was necessary on the part of Vaughan's brothers and sisters in smuggling letters to and from Nelle on the island. True love never did run smooth, so they say, and this was no exception, but they won through in the end. When Nelle sailed out to marry Vaughan in Bombay Cathedral in 1858, Vaughan's loyal sister, Emily, sailed with her as her chaperone, and signed the marriage register as a witness.

Apart from the many references which bring the people to life, it came as something of a surprise to find that Edward Robinson introduced red deer to Skomer in the 1850's. In later years, in the 1880's, when Vaughan Davies also rented Skokholm for a time, he put some of the deer down there as well. In one old, faded picture, taken on Skokholm, a red deer calf can be seen with Vaughan Davies scratching its head. It also came as a surprise to learn that at the same time there were hares on Skomer. They were fairly plentiful on the mainland, but I do not know of any other record of their having been introduced to the islands.

Vaughan Davies farmed on Skomer when times were good and, also towards the end of his tenure, when times were deplorable. He and his wife had six more children. One of the four boys, Walter, was drowned at sea, but the other three all seem to have done well in life following good educations. The three girls, who had a governess on the island before going away to finishing schools, all met their future husbands amongst the young men who visited Skomer.

When I wrote *The Sounds Between* I was marvellously fortunate in having access to a day-by-day diary which the late Ivor Arnold had kept during part of his time on Ramsey. I quoted considerable sections from those entries and many people were fascinated by them. I believe that the following passages will likewise speak to us from the past. To adapt the words of *The Flight of Ages* but slightly,

'For as long as the heart is beating,
As long as the eyes have tears,
We shall hear the echoes ringing
From out the golden years.'

June 15th, 1849—From Tom Robinson, staying at Broom Hill.

'Dear Vaughan,

Here I am, snug as a Bug in a Rug—except that a precious great flea is tormenting me, by mama Margaret Jones—I wrote to you some time ago, but from not having rec'd any answer, imagine the letter never came to hand. There's a tremendous clatter here, so, my old Cove, you must excuse incoherency. Last Tuesday week I went in company with your brothers & Co to Grassholm— we got there about 11.0 o'clock P.M. and Harry and myself waged an incessant war with the puffins &c &c until we left, which was not before 4.0 o'clock the next day. Our gents were in such a hurry to get away from the place that we were forced to start before the tide was with us, and with a fresh breeze from the N.E. and a smart 'jabble' we found ourselves in a fair way to reach the Cornish Coast. This would not pay so we put about and pulled up against the wind to clear Skomar Head, having effected which at the expense of much elbow grease, 'blessings'—(?) then hoisted the sail standing into the Bay hoping to fetch the North Haven were forced to go through with a heavy pull against tide before we set foot on Skomar—all of us rather the worse for wear—In consideration of this epistle and the —(?) I hope you will favour me with a long yarn containing all relating to yourself and ship— I'm in a great hurry so excuse this horrid scrawl and believe me to remain Dear Vaughan, Your most sincerely, T. M. Robinson.

I will write you at greater length in a few days, but my thoughts are gone wool gathering and I cannot collect them.'

July 17th, 1850. Letter from Harry (who signs himself 'Scrumpey') to Vaughan.

'Dear Twaney

It is six months since I last gave you a stem I had very good sport last winter in the frost and shot 9 woodcocks in one day at Hook with Tom we had only father's gun and Iris between us and he killed 3 besides John and Yanto went to Hoaten that day and they only killed 4 between Cor and him but next day he went with us and we bagged another 6 brace and 2 hares I am home for a week and do my best with the goosberries and hares although I have bad luck I have taken 3 in my springles on the Meadow hedge but the wire is too weak and has snapped each time I shot another at the pond but the gun did not do its work properly I was in the Island the first week of last month they are all well and Tom and his Gov'n got on very well Nelly was looking as good tempered as ever We caught the two blue falcons when I was in there Mr R— stuffed the both and the young one to make a case of. I am settled down to the lawyer's desk and get on very well as far as that goes and I like the dry stuff as well as I could like any profession— Haverford is very dull my only amusements are bathing and cricket I have no more news to tell but with best wishes for your bodily welfare

I remain &c

Scrumpey

P.S. I killed 26 woodcocks in all last winter Mr Robinson killed 27 in one day.'

[The word 'stem' in the Pembrokeshire dialect would normally be used in the sense to stem one's turn or take one's turn at a job. I have not previously heard it used in the sense in which Harry uses it here but he lived quite a bit before my time. 'Springle' was a snare. Originally it would have been made with a pliant stick and a noose of horse-hair, but obviously wire was already in use. Eventually snares became known as wires—R.H.]

Sept 14th, 1850—Letter from Mrs Emily Alicia Davies to her son Vaughan in which she tells him the sad news that his brother Richard had lost part of his foot as the result of an accident whilst threshing. No details are given, but he somehow caught his foot in the machine. The threshing machine at that time would have been in the barn and powered by a capstan type mechanism outside, with a pair of horses walking round and round on the old-fashioned 'horse course'. Another letter mentions that Roch was driving the horses at the time. Richard and Roch are the same person. He was the youngest of the large family, apart from the boy who had died in infancy, and was christened Richard David Roch. He would have been eighteen at the time of the accident and is often referred to also as Dick.

1851—No other date. Letter from Mrs Davies at Broom Hill to her son, 'My own dear Vaughan'

She speaks of domestic matters and then says that times are hard.

'Myra and I had a sad loss last night the rats carried away all our goslings 13 in number, but Dick had caught the old thief with a Ferret Mr Robinson gave use. John was in the Island last week they were all well and Tom talked of being out in May, he has not been out for twelve months the old Man and he do not hit it off exactly.'

Work has begun on the Fort on the Stack Rock and will shortly commence on the Point. Work is proceeding on the railway which will come to Milford—'it will be a great thing for this part of the world, and help in these sad Free Trade times which is nearly bringing all the Farmers to ruin.'

Everybody is saying they should grow Flax instead of Wheat or Barley.

[This letter was written in the decade following the repeal of the Corn Laws which meant that agricultural interests were now to be subservient to those of industry. Little did Mrs Davies realise it but the coming of the railway would also eventually herald the doom of so many rural trades and industries and also have their own deleterious effect on the prices of so much agricultural produce.—R.H.]

Feb 19th, 1853—Letter from Vaughan to Nelle. He is on the *Duke of Northumberland* on the Equator in Longitude 21 degrees.

Sister Myra is acting as a go-between. He is heading for Melbourne—'I think I shall go to the Diggings first of all, and if not lucky I shall either take to my old trade the sea again or some situation on shore.'

He did not go to the Diggings. He arrived at Port Phillip, along with his brother Tom, 'in company with five other ships crowded with emigrants. As soon as the ship was anchored we started for Melbourne to look for lodgings.'

This much we know from his own hand-written account which is amongst his papers. They found lodgings, but the carter who took their luggage said the standard charge was '5/- from the wharf to Flanders lane and one shilling more for every street as you come up the hill.'

Astounded that money could be made so easily, Vaughan immediately bought a horse and dray and set up in business in Melbourne. The horse cost £75 and the dray £50, but the horse 'turned out a jibber', so he sold him for £50 and bought a good horse for £120.

How he came out of the business eventually there is no knowing, but his sojourn does not seem to have lasted long before he went back to sea.

March 31st, 1854 'Bolly' to 'Twany'

'Times are very good upon farmers just now every thing selling, *very high*, barley £5 wheat 10 butter salt 13'd—beef & mutton 7'd & 8'd—I never remember such prices, a butcher came last week down from Swansea & bought & *paid* £100 worth with Papa without a dozen words to the bargain. We had one great loss, a fat cow got choked one night by the chain, but in other respects everything else seems to go smoothly—I often think how it would have gladdened dear Mamma's heart to see us now so completely above water, with the rent ready to the day & no fear of a bill coming in without the money to meet it, but I fervently trust she is in the enjoyment of far greater happiness above, and perhaps it would not have been safe for us to have all we wish for on earth, we should then be too happy & satisfied here and forget that better home above where I pray in God's own time we shall *all* yet meet & enjoy a happiness which care & death can never come to mar.'

(Their mother had died two years earlier on March 18th 1852—R.H.)

On April 17th, 1854, 'Bolly' wrote to 'Twany' and referred to the fact that he had been shipwrecked and had come through it with renewed Faith and Trust.

Oct 30th, 1854 'Bolly' to 'Twany'

Brother Tom has returned from Australia and there is bad feeling between them at Broom Hill. There is reference to how she misses her mother, and then—'I met the old governor of Skomar in Haverford last week, he told me the two girls were come home quite well & 'delighted to find themselves once more back'!! I said 'of course, there's no place like Home' & thought in my own mind it was to be hoped there were not many places like theirs.'

March 12th, 1855—From brother Charley, home at Broom Hill, to Vaughan.

'There was a large steamer wrecked on the South Bishop in a fog about three weeks ago. I believe ten lives were lost out of 80—one boat landed on the Island and Mr Robinson sent them on shore, there has been several things picked up about the coast and I have no doubt the 'Old Man' kept his eyes open to all strays passing

The Derrick for winching up the cliff from South Haven.

through the sound. I understand he has made a great deal of money this year on his rabbits. Mr Summers on Ramsey tried the same dodge but I believe he barely paid the expence of catching them.'

[The term 'sent', used here in the context that Mr Robinson had sent them on shore, is probably used in the old Pembrokeshire sense of the term 'to send somebody', meaning to accompany them part of the way.—R.H.]

May 15th, 1855. From Charley, at Brighton, to Vaughan—

'I went into Skomer Island 3 days before I left home and I brought in the 'Israelite' and introduced him to the Fair Islanders as luck would have it Master Tom was coming out as I went in the old man was walking out looking out for some wreck of the 'Morna' wrecked off the Bishops and Nelly had a good look at the Bearded man and knew him immediately but did not dare take possession as Miss Annie is the Old Man's spy. I also brought in a chit from Pye which I secretly delivered to Nelly asking her to say Twaney whether she had entirely forgotten you and I believe she is *True Blue* from the answer she sent to Pye and which I believe has been sent to you by the April Mail. Nelly was looking much thinner than when I saw her last. I took dinner there and the Old Man was the very essence of politeness and so very pressing upon me to remain over night and he would put me out in his own boat next day. He could not make out your likeness at all but something like Warren Davies which I suppose you ought to take as a compliment. The Old fellow has been very successful with his Rabbit trade this year and appeared in high feather he has introduced 4 deer from Essex into the Island and talks soon of supplying the London Market in Rabbits. Tom is grown a fine tall fellow and a little whisker improves him very much and he does not look so long necked as he used to but I cannot say there is much moral improvement to be discovered. The Old Gentleman appears to give him a little more longitude than he used to do and I believe Tom makes himself very useful in taking out and catching the Rabbits he has been out in a heavy boat 3 times a week all through the winter with never more than two men with him and very often only one which is hard work as you may easily imagine and not the most agreeable cruising ground is the Jack Sound.'

One interesting point in this letter is that Charley said he had brought in the 'Israelite' and also 'brought in a chit.' In Pembrokeshire we just do not know the difference between bring and take. I have an idea he should have written, 'I took in.' But don't take my word for it.

Of more general interest, perhaps, is the fact that 'Miss Annie' was Edward Robinson's other daughter, Nelly's elder sister. And we know, too, that it was round about that time that Vaughan had grown the beard which he kept to the end of his days.

There is another letter, undated, but it must have been round about that time, from Dick to Vaughan, who had sent a picture of himself with a beard. Dick said he ought to send one to Nelly—

'I saw her sister the other day she said she was quite well. We asked them here, as they were staying at Trewarren, but they did not honour us. The old man is making a capital thing of his rabbits 2/4 per couple. He says he shall clear £500 this year by them.'

June 17th, 1856 . From 'Bolly' to 'Twany'

'I write this chit to Calcutta to say that Pye heard from Nelle, she has been greatly puzzled poor girl, as we have indeed all been as to the best mode of proceedings. Knowing so little of Mr Robinson as we do, Myra & I could not judge what was best to advise her or what chance she had of persuading her Papa; & it appears from her decision not to give your letter that she does not feel she had much influence neither can she reckon in any way on Annie for assistance or sympathy & has never ventured to tell her how matters stand though she evidently suspects by her constant questioning Nelle, that Nelle hears more of your movements than *she* knows. I am very sorry for the poor child, not even to have her sister to advise well but I think she has done right, indeed I may say I am *sure* she has, because she prayed for God's direction, & so did we all, I know full well that He hears and answers *all* that come unto Him in faith; & I have no doubt your way will be made clear as soon as ever He sees it will be good for you both. She seems to wish to defer the final answer until you have something definite to propose, just to wait in case the Arrow should be sold to see when you would next be due, because that in the meantime you can hear of her and she of you as you do now & perhaps her Papa would be more likely to give his consent if he saw a certain prospect than allow her to engage herself to an uncertainty. If you think you have enough to maintain a wife *she* thinks so too, but perhaps her Papa might not—now from upon the three children have their Mother's property settled on *them* not *on him* & of course now they are of age they have a right to claim it, but as he lives upon it now, he does not wish to have the subject broached, & he of course thinks that if you were to marry Nelly you would ask what he could give her, for judging other people *by himself* he would never believe anyone to be so simple as not to care about money, but if you should be able to come home in fixed command, or get a permanent appointment out there, & be able to take Nelle for herself alone perhaps he will let her go. *She* is quite willing to go to India, or anywhere & though if she were *my* daughter I should be very sorry to see her go so far, yet I think he cares for little besides his own comfort, he is a terribly selfish man & provided it *does* not interfere with *his* comfort he seems to care little about his children.

I hope dear old fellow you won't feel cast down by this further trial of your patience, it will all come right by & bye—"All things work together for *good* to them that *love* God"—try both of you to be of that happy band, then no harm can come, a year or two will soon pass away when rightly employed & she is really I think worth waiting for & if you can't come home to fetch her out I will chaperone her out rather than she shall want for one; but I hope you and old Dunbar will make up a match & that you will come home to live.'

Dear old Bolly. Does not the heart warm to her after all these years, even though we never knew her? In the event, she did, a couple of years later, sail with Nelle to India and signed the register when Vaughan and Nelle were married in Bombay Cathedral. Surely she is happy with all of them in that Heaven of which she always spoke so confidently.

August 1st, 1856 From Dick to Twaney.

'I have been conveying Tom Robinson all the summer in Warren Davies's boat. Although poor fellow he is not to be envied now the old man has been treating him so bad of late; that last week he left the old brute; and says that he shall go to sea I think it will be the best thing for him as he is got to old to be treated as a child. What do you think of being called a D--d *unprincipald scoundrel* because he stayed out one day longer than he should have done at Rickeston. Tom is I think a much better fellow than he was. At any rate he has a good heart. He says that he is going to London and means to go before the mast to the south seas. But Tom (that would be brother Tom—R.H.) recommended him to go to India as he was sure you would do what you could for him.'

On Oct 16th, 1856, Bolly wrote to Vaughan begging him to come home and saying money wasn't everything. On the farm the crops are good and all well saved. Then in the middle of all the domesticity and personal considerations, there is a delightful letter from a gentleman, of indecipherable signature, writing from Singapore.

Oct 29th, 1856, to Capt V. P. Davies of the Brig. 'Arrow'.

'My Dear Captain Davies,

Herewith I send for bearer one Tortoise with an empty Tub which please receive on board together with one Trunk of wearing apparel & one bag of Pearl Sagoe, The Tortoise you will please put in Tub with a salt water, the water to be changed every day and if you will do so I think no doubt it will reach in Bombay in safety as it is for the use of Mr Dosabloy Coma, who has written to me to give you in charge. The Tortoise as soon as you receive on board please to order to put him in a tub, and let the Tub be first filled up with salt water and by so doing shall be much obliged.

Yours truly

P. Restonge (?)'

In a letter of January 1857 there is a reference to Vaughan's formal proposal and then, on December 24th, 1857, Bolly wrote a long letter to Pye. Bolly was on board the ship 'Pekin' in the Red Sea on her way to Bombay with Nelle for the wedding.

Dec 8th '58—Letter from Edward Robinson on Skomer Island to Nelly.

'My dearest Nelly

Not having any thin paper I must write a few lines on common notepaper knowing you would rather have them so than not at all. I received a note from Annie telling me she was going to send a letter to you & if I would send a few lines she would enclose them, so without having any thing particular to communicate I take my pen in hand to tell you what is going on here. Annie will no doubt tell you everything else. We are going on much as usual rabbit killing being the chief object at this time of year claims my attention most. The man I have in Kent's place I do not think anything like so good a trapper as Kent, nor do I think so many rabbits will be killed by some hundreds if not thousands as I sent away last tho' there are more rabbits I believe by a very great many than last year they are getting up to trap. The herd of deer is increasing & they are looking well. They now number fifteen.

Topsy is quite well and all the rest of the pets. Busy now enjoys herself with the trappers. Jock is getting very old & shows his age very much. Still he continues to accompany me in my daily walks but if I stop to look at the trappers he lays down, I do not see him, & go away giving him a call which he is too deaf to hear, so at last he wakes up, finds I am gone & toddles home. Mifs Wilkins sent in on Sunday last for a couple of rabbits, she could get plenty of rabbits about the place but it was Skomer rabbits she wanted, of course I sent her out a couple but from what I hear the poor thing would hardly be able to taste them, she has I believe been sinking for a long time. You may have heard of the death of Rev'd W. Roch. It seems he never really rallied after the death of his nephew young George of Butter Hill. The absence of our kind friends the Warren Davises is a sad affair for me. I heard from Mr D. last week, they seem to be very comfortable & I expect the pleasure of seeing him soon after Xmas. I have not been out of the Island since the end of Sept. Businefs will I expect call me out next week but I have now nothing to tempt' me out, Trewarren being empty & just now Annie being out my time is fully occupied. I expect her home soon after Xmas & Johnny with her. She told me she was going with Mrs Lowndes to get another outfit for you, which outfit it seems was for an expected arrival. May God prosper you my dear child & give you a happy issue out of all your troubles and dangers. Mrs Lowndes says she shall expect to see me two inches higher in consequence of being a Grand papa: Give my love to Vaughan & with very much love & affection to yourself believe me ever my dearest Nelly Your very affect'n Father

Edward Robinson.'

There is an undated letter from Annie to Nelly, but it would have been round about the winter of 1858, or the spring of 1859, because Nelly is expecting.

'Rabbit killing is not over yet, the number is not killed yet, not more than 6,000 as yet. One of the bucks was found dead, from fighting it is supposed.'

[Does this suggest that Edward Robinson, like other islanders are known to have done, introduced bucks to improve the strain?

There are 'throw-backs' to many varying types of rabbits on all the islands. R.H.]

There is another undated letter of about the same time from Annie to Nelly,

'Ann today is busy salting two pigs which were killed yesterday. Very likely their hams will go out to you. Jim is rabbit catching this winter, he thought of going to sea but I suppose he fancied trapping better. Old Billy Dawkins is still here & Tom Stevens, who was here the year before last. Hannah is remarkably stupid, she seemed to have learnt all she can & that is little enough, she is very careless, they none of them improve much on acquaintance. How do you get on with your servants? Have you any European or are they natives?'

The Ann referred to in this letter is probably Ann Lush who was born in the Isle of Wight and came with the Robinsons to Skomer. Ellin or Nelly, the youngest of the three children, was also born in the Isle of Wight. In the spring of 1859 she wrote to Nelly herself.

Also in 1859, but otherwise undated, there is the copy of a notice issued by Edward Robinson warning trespassers off Skomer, Midland, the Garland Stone and Mew Stone. There is no indication of what was happening, but it was a time when there was much activity on the part of those who took sea-birds for their wings, which were used as decorations in ladies' hats.

March 15th, 1859. From Annie to Nelly.

'I must soon begin gardening—I expect a lot of plants from Priests, & hope my garden will be very gay this summer. The tiresome hares have eaten up all my carnations. We have two nice broods of chickens, did I tell you that all the white ducks are gone but one. The cows laid upon one in the shed & demolished the poor thing & the old lame duck went long ago. The two old turkeys are killed and sold. We are not going to rear any more, so now all my imoluments are gone, unless the bees bring me in a few dollars.'

'The hams are most of them smoked but not dry enough to send abroad as yet. I hope you will find them as good as the last. Papa went down to the pond last week & shot a pair of Shoveller ducks, very rare birds. So as they were nicely killed he skinned them yesterday and thinks of setting them up today. The drake is the most beautiful bird of the duck tribe I ever saw—the duck is like a wild duck in plumage but with most peculiar bills flattened at the end like a shovel, so when you & Vaughan pay us a visit I hope there will be a new case for you to see. Do you ever get crabs and lobsters in your part of the world? I should much like to know. The men have begun fishing here but I think they have not had any startling catches yet. We have had some crabs and pollock off Folland, quite a treat. You know we are such lovers of fish.'

April 12th, 1859. From Annie to Nelly.

—'This morning my old duck was brought up with 5 young ones, but they appear very weak. We have 29 chicks and a nice brood of 9 ducks good big ones & some more are expected on Saturday but as they are Topper's eggs I am doubtful of them. My geese have laid 8 eggs between them and left off, so I am waiting for the turkey to set to give them to her.'

'Papa has begun sending out sheep 2 a week & Martha Edwards sells them in Milford & we have sold a pot of butter & last week we sent some eggs & another pot of butter is going this week.'

'I am going to write to Tom about a wooden beehive. If I get one I will let you know how it answers, it is to save killing the bees.'

April 27th 1859—From Ann to Nelly

'My dear Nelly

Annie tells that she must send her letter out next Monday so I thought if I was to write to you at the same time I had better look sharpe about it or I do not think you will get one from me this time but I wanted to write this male to congratulate on your safety after your late illnefs and of the safe arrival of your small son which I truly hope at this time both he and his Mamma is flourishing you do not know how very glad I was when I heard that your Husband was with you in your illnefs you would have been so very lonely without him at that time I am sure if wishing could have made him stay with you at that time he had plenty of them from home last Saturday we heard the news Folland came early on purpos so when your Papa came in doors he was saying *news, news,* news I thought, I wonder what it is then out came your dad with a glafs

Capt. Vaughan Palmer Davies (right) and his men washing sheep.

of gin for Folland did not know what the matter was then
presently it came out that the gin was to drink the safe arrival of
his grandson and I am quite sure if the little one do not thrive
properly it will not be for the want of good wishes the all wished
mifs Annie joy of her nephew. I have got a little bit to tell you of
annie you must know your Papa have been drinking ale for his tea
of an evening lately and he had some on Saturday evening so
when your dad was gone up to Bead Annie says I wonder why
father did not have any grog tonight I think he ought to have had
some tonight to drink nellys health with you dont you, I laughed
untill I was weak at her for she was wanting some herself and she
never got any when I went to fetch the candle I tould your Papa
but he did not say she might have some so she went to bed
without any I tould her I would tell you when wrote she called me
a ninn do you remember Mr Williams the Doctor of Milford he is
dead and Mr Pratt of Hwest, two of the years calves had died laitly
all the different kinds of birds are come we have rather good luck
with the Poultry this season there is as many as 90 chickings and

46 Ducks one of the Turkeys is siting on 6 of Annie's gose eggs that is all the geese have lade yet do not know if they mean to finish after that. Topsy is quite well at least she was on Sunday and just as fat as ever Mr and Mrs W-Davis have been home for a week thay are gone again I believe Mr D. came for the rents little Busey and Jock and Pilot are all very well your Papa and Annie are both very well and thay live on all kinds of daintey things as for Annie she is getting quite fat since she came home from London its my beliefs thay did not give her enough to eat while she was there.

I will now wish you adue with all the happynefs you deserve in this wourld and I think that is a lot and my best love and believe me to be your old friend ann. please to remember me very kindly to Mr Davis and tell him I wish him joy of his sone'

Shortly after the birth of the first baby, who was named Charles Edward, and who was the only one of the seven children not born during the time on Skomer, we come to the affair of when and why Vaughan Davies gave up his life at sea.

On December 23rd, 1859, Vaughan's brother, Charley, wrote to him from on board the S.S. *Norna*

'I am delighted to hear by the last home news that your old craft had arrived safely at Liverpool and I hope ere this reaches Broom Hill that you are down there old boy having a peep at the Old folks at home, I saw Nelly's chit to Miss Flower from St Helena with all the Cape adventures and was glad to hear that you were all well in health although the weather must have been very trying to poor Nelly and the Royal Charlie.'

I think that passage of that letter, although taken out of chronological order, was worth quoting because it shows the state of the vessel Vaughan Davies was bringing home to Liverpool, and also it adds weight to the story as told to me by his grandson, the late Edward Scriven.

Tom Robinson, Nelly's brother, had written to her from London in the November. It was a cheerful letter in which he referred to the weather on their voyage home and asked. 'Who is Forman?' It was, as the saying goes, a good question.

There is no point in quoting all the correspondence involved, but the first references go back to the April of 1859 when Forman entered into an agreement with Vaughan Davies to bring his ship the 'Princess Somawatty' to Liverpool. He clearly stated his intention to sell the ship on arrival, if he could receive a very good offer, and, in this event, would pay Vaughan Davies his overland return fare to Bombay.

The ship having reached Liverpool safely, no doubt to the owner's surprise and disappointment, the wrangling started. Throughout the long drawn-out affair Forman comes through as a thoroughly nasty piece of work, of whom the kindest thing that could be said was that, as we say in Pembrokeshire, he wanted the bean for the pea every time. Having worked as a journalist for a similar sort of firm my sympathies are all with Vaughan Davies. Nelly returned to Skomer, and Vaughan stayed on in lodgings whilst he fought his battle with Forman and Forman's agent, Kingcombe, and tried for a new ship. He was, in fact, trying for a new ship until well on in 1860.

He turned for advice to E. K. Bridger, an old friend of the family in London, who was to become a frequent visitor to Skomer. Bridger wrote of the possibility, and of the need, of taking legal action to prevent Forman leaving the country before the affair had been settled, and also from selling the ship before the captain had been paid.

Forman had put him on half-pay and, when Vaughan Davies refused to accept this, he had been dismissed and demanded a month's wages. His full claim, including the return fare to India as agreed, was for £190. The letters to his wife show much of his sterling character, integrity and love of family. Eventually, on January 3rd 1860, he wrote to say that, in order to avoid legal costs, he had agreed to settle. In the agreement he signed it said, 'Received from Mr Kingcombe on account of Captain Forman owner of the ship 'Princess Somawatty' One hundred and twenty pounds eleven shillings being the amount I agreed to take in my letter of Dec 28th to throw up command and all claim on the owners of the above ship in full settlement of wages and passage money to Bombay.'

When he was able to write to tell Nelly of the outcome he said they must now forgive the deceitful people who had used them so badly and put themselves in God's hands.

Yes, his daily service of prayer would have been very significant in his life. Indeed, back in 1855, he had been in danger of losing command of his ship because he had refused to make the crew work on Sundays.

Whilst all this had been going on Annie had written to Nelly, on June 2nd, 1859.

She began the letter by saying how excited they were at the news that Vaughan and Nelly would be coming home in the spring. She spoke of the uncertainty of communicating with friends on shore and also of those who had visited them on the Island. And then,

'I have a young Falcon to bring up, it was brought from the nest yesterday & is in the coop in the garden. I intend to call him Joey. I think Frank Stackpoole wants one.'

'Papa wishes very much that Vaughan would be good enough to try and get some large Malay fowls & bring home when you come. He wants the heaviest birds, not those with long legs and small bodies. If you can manage to bring him home some fine cocks & hens he will be very much pleased & obliged.'

'We have a swarm of poultry, more than 100, mostly ducks. My geese eggs were all failures.'

'All our nice dogs are well, but old Jock is failing fast. I shall be very sorry when he is gone, you know he was a great pet of mine.'

'The meadow sweet is just coming in flower and soon I hope I shall have lots of pretty things in my garden.'

It will have been noted that poultry on Skomer were a considerable enterprise and, of course, the island was free of such predators as foxes, rats, stoats and weasels, with all of which the poultry keeper on the mainland would have had to contend. There were only the falcons, and their likely depredations need to be borne in mind when reading of their being taken from the nest.

Whilst the wrangle with Forman had been going on, he and his agent, Kingcombe, had done their best to blacken Vaughan Davies' name all round Liverpool and amongst seafaring people.

Then, the affair having been settled, they did their best to persuade him to take command of another of their ships.

On January 9th, 1861, however, E. K. Bridger wrote to Vaughan to say,

'I am delighted to hear that it is positively settled that your are to have Skomer & thank you much for your kind invitation which I sincerely hope some day or other to be able to accept for I have ever since I first saw it longed to spend a few days there. It is the most romantic spot I have ever seen and when the birds are there the most wonderful sight in creation.'

The letter is not dated but, shortly before Vaughan Davies took over, he wrote to Edward Robinson,

'Dear Mr Robinson,

If there is any chance of your procuring a house before Lady Day I think it would be better for me to take the Island from the 1st January and have the stock and crops valued at once but

Puffins above South Haven in the 1880's.

should you determine to keep it on for the Half year of course it will alter the case in the event of your doing so. I would much prefer your disposing of your fat stock and such ...(?) That will not be required for the house, and in fact anything you think I had better not keep on for by selling to the Dealers you will be more likely to get the proper value than by having them valued. If I am to take it on from the 1st January I think we had better dispense with old Margaret Lewis particularly if we can make an agreement with Jim to stay after the rabbit season is over. I have no objection to give him the same as Kent had if he likes to stay with me.'

January 30th, 1861. Vaughan Davies to Edward Robinson

'My dear Mr Robinson,

I did not expect you out on Thursday consequently did not go to Marloes to see you. I received Annie's note respecting the barley as well as one from Hassel and will of course add the amount to the end of the inventory. We came in on Friday and have had a little time to ...(?) I would never have believed there are so many things about the place had I not seen them. I was surprised to see in the inventory Sundries in the granary £6 but I must confess I think they are fully worth it.'

Following this there was a letter from Annie from which it appeared there had been some misunderstanding over some of the furniture and cases of birds. This was sorted out, and then came more trouble, as a copy of a letter from Vaughan Davies to his father-in-law indicates.

'My dear Mr Robinson,

I am sure you will be greatly surprised at some unpleasantness which I have to communicate respecting Jim. Saturday being too wet to set he asked me for £1 and permission to go out to get some boots promising to come in again on Sunday. I asked Anne (probably Anne Lush—R.H.) whether it would be proper to let him go out and she said she thought it would as he had no boots, so I let him go and he never came in again until this afternoon Wednesday, his excuse was that he had a bad throat (which I am much inclined to doubt).

After Jim left on Saturday George took Maida out to kill rabbits and she caught a hare. I therefore ordered him not to take her out

again as I particularly wished to preserve the hares. When Jim
came in this afternoon he took Maida away with him. I told him
also not to take her out as I was afraid she would kill the hares
when he told me in the most insolent manner that he would take
her whenever he liked, he said that I had nothing whatsoever to
do with him that you give him orders/I don't care if you do not let
me have the dog I will go out tomorrow and you can catch the
rabbits how you can and I will tell Mr Robinson that you sprung
the traps and be damned to you. So then I made enquiries of
George about the traps being sprung and he said that three had
been sprung on Lowercot Ruck Dumble where a lamb was caught
by the leg and believed I had sprung one in getting the lamb out
and I ordered George to be careful to set tham well in the holes or
the lambs would be caught again. Now Mr Robinson I shall be
obliged by your letting me know by return what I am do do as I
shall not permit Jim to come to the Island till I hear from you—to
prevent any further dispute about the dog I will send her out of
the Island.'

We cannot be certain of Jim's identity but it sounds very much
as if it would have been Jim Evans, known in later years as 'Jim the
Hunter.' If so, everything would seem to have been satisfactorily
settled. Vaughan Davies took over officially on Lady Day 1861,
Jim Evans married a Marloes girl in 1864 and he remained as an
ever present on Skomer until 1891.

From this time on there are not many letters and those which
are of interest are mainly from the children whilst away at school.
There was, however, one more from 'Bolly' at Broom Hill to her
brother Harry, who was now a solicitor at Hastings.

Oct 12th, 1864.

'Dearest Hal

We want your opinion upon a point of law so answer this *at once*.
You ought to have been told all the exciting details by Cor or
Roch, & I have urged them to send a history of their proceedings
to you knowing what a seal catcher you are, but they have been to
lazy, & I have been to poorly & too busy since to have time, so I
can only give outlines, they must fill up the Picture. On Saturday
week Roch telegraphed to Cor Cole to come down to go to

Grasholm on Monday the 3rd—he came, & Roch, Cor, Folland & Dick went. From the time we got up it blew very hard from the East, early in the day it increased to a heavy gale, which continued all day Tuesday. We never dreamt they went further than Skomar & felt satisfied about them—on Wednesday morning we heard from Marloes that they had gone to Grasholm & were *not in Skomar*. It was then blowing *strong* from the East still; John was away for the week with the young lady, Vaughan in the Island with *no Boat*, & noboby but Pye & me to act—we instantly sent off Jones the Griffin to get a Pilot Boat to go out to see if they were on Grasholm, & if the *Boat could* not go, he was to get a *Steamer*. He came back and said the Pilot boat *was going off when he left*; that the men said it was *pofsible* they might not be able *to take them* off the Island that night, but they would stand by them all night & take them off the first thing on Thursday morn. Meanwhile Vaughan came out by himself (& Jim) *in the Duke* that afternoon, to say that he saw a flag on Grasholm & to send out a smack as no doubt they had lost their Boat & *went back* at once, as Nelly was in Solva. We were tolerably easy expecting the smack would bring them in about 10 or ll at night (for by six o'clock the wind had *become quite calm*— Thursday morning came no signs of the smack, or of the men—The Marloes men sent down to ask Jones should they go in then; he said '*No* the smack has them by this time'—As the day wore away we got terribly uneasy, & sent up to Marloes to engage one of their Boats to go, & sent up provisions fearing they might be on the rock starving—We then sent off a man to Neyland to try to get a Steamer & Vaughan *again came out* to say no time must be lost they might be perishing with cold and hunger as this was *the fourth day*—He then went out to St Annes to Telegraph for the Lightening(?) and when he got there the smack was just coming round the head at 6 o'clock on Thursday *evening*. She never tried to go at all on Wednesday, never went out to them till *12 o'clock* on Thursday (though the wind was due East all the time, & so moderate that the three Marloes Boats went to Skokholm & back on *Wednesday & Thursday*, would not stop to take off the Boat or any of their chattels) and had the conscience to charge £10 for their trip! Jones made *no* bargain with them, & had they gone on

Wednesday & tried to save them we should have been too thankful to have paid even that exorbitant charge, but I consider that they failed to fulfil their engagement & they have no *claim* on us for their work on Thursday, because in consequence of their non appearance I had *engaged a Marloes* Boat & had it not been for the Telegraph the *Steamer* would have been engaged at Neyland— However we found from the crew that they attend the Smalls & the Bishops for 3,,10,,0 a trip; & *The Mumbles*, & Cardigan 5,,0,,0 a trip—So Cor went up yesterday & offered them 3,,10,,0 for their day's work, they refused, & he then offered from Roch & himself a sovereign each, making 5..10..0 (for what the Marloes Boat would have done for £1) but they refused, & would not take a penny lefs than £10..0..0 and we want to know whether there is Law to force us to pay. There are plenty of seafaring people here to prove that there was *nothing to prevent* their going out on Wednesday: only we discovered that they were expecting a *steam tug* to pilot in, so no doubt they waited for her, & when it became clear enough on Thursday morning to see she was not on the horizon *then*, & *not till then* they started. They even went so far as to tell Roch that they *had* lost a Steam tug & a Vefsel by going out—that the tug was £7-10- & the Vefsel 3..0..0—& *so* they thought £10 about a fair charge—but when they landed at St Annes their first question was 'Any Vefsels gone in since we left?' & the answer, 'No, not one'—so they have not spoken of them since—Let us know whether we can defend this charge with succefs. It was inhuman their not going out, & might have cost the poor fellows their *lives as it* was they did not want afsistance & could have got from there themselves the following day—Their story is, that it looked doubtful at six o'clock on Monday still they hoped it would clear up—, started at 7, a splended wind and tide; at 8 wind began to rise & the sea, & Folland said 'Let us turn back,' they tried; but it was impossible! Nothing was left but to run before the hurricane—The sail was carried away, & for six hours they pulled for life without making an inch, merely trying to keep themselves from going further away/for by this time they were nearing the Smalls & to complete the horror of their position the sea caught the oar out of Folland's hand & broke one of his ribs—at last the tide turned, & though the wind was higher than ever, Hope gave them fresh courage to strive for life, & by God's great mercy, after 10 hours pulling they reached the Island *safe!* drenched to the skin of course all their blankets & food saturated, poor Cor's wrist skinned for quarter of a yard in Baling out the water and—you may guefs Roch's hand pulling—They were able to pull up their Boat but were to exhausted to do anything else but creep into a damp shelving cave, out of the wind, try to light a fire, & lie down wet & miserable. Roch says it was almost as hopelefs as the Sea. But next day they rigged up a tent, took off their clothes and dried them, cut grafs for a bed, shared out their prov so that they arranged enough to keep them *alive for a week* & as poor Folland was preserved from Inflamation, *they* were fairly off, ony troubled about the anxiety we were in—It was very unfortunate, for had they gone the week before last it was lovely & fine, & this week equally so—Cor is gone to Skomer today, hoping for Woodcocks but none have been yet seen, Charlie is I suppose this week in London, he has to prove the charge against the Captain of the 'Granada' a very unpleasant businefs, all are well here except me, & mine is my old attack made worse by the fright—Tom at Gloster *hoping*—Give us an answer at once—had we better defend the charge if they push it. With best love Yr Very affec Bolly'

As is so often the case there is no record of the eventual outcome. There is, however, a copy of a letter from H. G. R. Davies to a Mr Stokes, presumably a legal associate, asking for an opinion. He recounts the details of the episode and suggests his interpretation of the law. Amongst other things he wrote, 'If they sue my brother who gave the order the case is one for the County Court but if they can sue the Younger one for work done &c this may be a case for the superior Courts as one of the party was a Gent'n from Carmarthenshire.

I have no common law books here to look up these points as we do no common law & my old Father does not want to go to law or be imposed on.'

I doubt very much, somehow, whether the gentlemen of the Smack would have gone to law.

One advantage Vaughan Davies had during his time farming on Skomer was the fact that his brother, Tom, was farming at East Hook, a farm between Martinshaven and Marloes, and known at that time as Hook. The farm had been in the possession of the family for some time, and Dick, or Roch, had spent time there when he was younger. He remained a bachelor and would seem to have had some regrets. He wrote in the Skomer 'writing album', when he visited there in 1889 at the age of fifty-eight,

'A Batcherlor born
All women to scorn
But now he is old and grey
And for that scorn he has to pay.'

The benefit to Vaughan Davies of having a brother at Hook was the fact that he could house stock there on the way to or from livestock fairs at Haverfordwest and he, or members of his family, could stay there overnight when the need arose.

During the 1880's he also rented Skokholm for the grazing but, for the most part, nobody lived there during that time, except when they were catching the rabbits, or perhaps for the occasional night when tending the stock. In addition to having a boat of their own on the island they also relied on the Marloes boatmen, particularly old Richard Edwards, known as Dick the Lane, and his son William.

So then, we come to the few remaining letters, the 'writing album' which became a visitors' book, and four little diaries which Mrs Davies kept during the 1880's.

Feb 9th, 1878. Clara, who sometimes signed herself Claire, from Leighton College. Writing of one of the girls,

'Her father is a barrister and I fancy not very well off, something like ourselves.'

Aug 3rd, 1878. Charlie writing from Carmarthen where he worked in the Brecon Old Bank,

'I am very sorry to hear of the great loss Papa had in all those sheep being killed in the last storm we never had any in Carmarthen.'

Three generations of boatmen Richard Edwards ["Old Dicky"]
his son William Edwards and grandson "Young Dicky").

Oct 21st, 1878. From Charlie at Carmarthen.
'How are the rabbits turning out this year I do hope you will get
a good catch as you have been getting so few every year of late.'
Nov 16th, 1878. Howard writing to his mother, from school,
'The young seal is a very expensive one Papa says it drinks 3
quarts of milk a day. I think it was time that uncle Harry came for
it.'
May 7th, 1879. Charlie from Carmarthen,
'I was very glad to receive your letter though am sorry to hear of
your loss in the farm as poor Papa has been very unfortunate with
everything this year though hope he may be able to make up for
it in something else yet the fact of there being no grass does not
look very promising for a large catch of rabbits which I hope he
may have.'
Aug 26th, 1883. From Harvey at Monmouth School,
'When you get this letter will you send me a lot of eggs. Birds
eggs I mean.'.

Sept 15th, 1886. From Harvey on Skokholm Island,
'Dearest Mother,
I received your letter and clothes quite safely yesterday and the
biscuits & fowl. I send off today 157 couple of rabbits in 2 of
DG.S. and 3 of our own we are going to set the old head setting
today and that will be about half way round. I am going to write
to Aunt Annie tonight. Give my best love to all on the Island.
Please send us some clear fat or lard to fry our spuds Jim says he
wants to see the Dad down here and may be his gun to work some
of his traps . . .(?) so as to catch the rabbits in a corral on the neck.
Love for yourself I remain Your loving son Harvey.
Please send second vol of Monte Christo and 3 vol if you have
got it & some mustard.'
Dec 5th, 1887 From Vaughan on Skomer to his brother, Harry.
'Dear Harry
I am glad you are going to take Kates money for since the
Warwick Bank affair we dont know who to trust—I have given the
bank notice of withdrawal and will send you a cheque of Draft
between this and the new year—sooner if your require it.
I am sorry to hear that you are not so well—you must take more
care of yourself—we are not so young as we were and I find I
cannot work as I did some years ago—where are you going for
Christmas if you have no better place in view come away down
here You know there is no place like this for setting you up—I have
only seen 1 woodcock this year but there are 2 hen pheasants on
the Island—Roch is going to give me a cock when he come down
next—I should like to have a couple of brace of grouse to see if
they would breed here where could I get them. The rabbits are
doing very badly this season not half a crop and the price low.
Things were looking well on Skokholm last week. I saw some very
large snipe there and they lay very well I wish I had taken the
gun—
We heard from the girls this morning they appear very happy
You must bring down another crew next summer that Clair may
have a chance—but I shall not let her go unless you bring a *very*
elligible young man—when my girls are all gone I shall invite some

of the outside girls and charge a commission which we can share. Nelle and Clair send best love.'

The 'writing album' was, unfortunately, not given to Mrs Davies until July, 1888, which was near to the end of their time on the island. Even so, apart from the interesting family references and showing the parties who visited Skomer, there are a few entries of more general interest.

Oct 2nd, 1888. C. F. Davies 'Goodby dear little Dickies I can't kill any more of you this time.'

Sept 11th-12th, 1899. Henry F. W. Harries and Thos E. Harries, Llandaff.

'A most enjoyable visit & shoot thanks to the great kindnefs of all at Skomer:

22 Brace Partridges 1 Duck.'

May 22nd, 1890. John Oldham, Southam.

'120 eggs this day.'

Capt. and Mrs. Vaughan Palmer Davies with their family and visiting friends.

May 17th-24th, 1891. Walter Taylor, Manchester.
'Saw first green eggs 20th.'
   Jan 5th, 1892. E. Scriven, Harpole.
'Came for a weeks shooting to clear up remains.
Bag. 3 Cocks, 12 Pheasants
11 Partridges, 11 Snipe
1 Teal 1 Plover & 23 Rabbits.'
Jan 13th, 1892. W. Edwardes, St. Brides.
'15 Woodcock 3 Snipe.'
Last of all we come to the diaries of Mrs Davies and, if such a
thing could be possible, they are of even more interest than the
letters. There are only four of them and, again, for a period
nearing the end of the Davies tenure of Skomer so that there is no
record of their affairs when farming prospered. The diaries are for
the years 1884, '5, '7 & '8. The entries are all brief and many days
have no entries at all. There are also periods when Mrs. Davies
was way from home visiting her family. There are constant
references to the weather, because it played such a big part in the
lives of island—bound people who were waiting for a boat with
letters or supplies or, perhaps, because stock were ready to go to
the fair, as the mart was then known.

   Eliza Stevens of Marloes, whose picture fetching water from the
well is familiar to many, was not, as had been supposed, a full-
time worker on the island, but went over for periods when she
was needed, such as at harvest time or feathering the poultry
ready for Christmas. There are also brief, but fascinating,
references to such rural matters as the hiring fairs. Indeed there is
so much which speaks to us in those little entries of life on the
island, and the life of that generation, that it is a formidable task
to know what to omit.

1884
W. June 18th	We all went out to Marloes Sands.
Th June 19th	So hot we went out in the boat with Walter.
Th July 3rd	A fine day they all played lawn tennis.
M Aug 18th	Eliza came in.
W ,, 20th	Vaughan Jim & the boys took 6 ponies to Skokholm.
Th ,, 28th	Vaughan & the boys out with the first freight of rabbits

Eliza. (Lisha) Stevens fetching water from the well.

Sat ,,30th	Vaughan & the boys took out 2 cattle. Blowing fresh.
W Sept 3rd	Busy getting everything ready for Skokholm.
Th ,, 4th	Jim, Walter & Harvey went down to Skokholm.
F ,, 5th	Dick came over and took out three colts. Vaughan out. finished binding barley.
S ,, 13th	The blacksmith came in. Sent over three pots butter.
F ,, 19th	Harvey went to school.
Sat Sept 27th	Howard left us for sea.

Milking time. The flag pole in the background was used for signalling to the Boathouse on the mainland. [See "The Sounds Between"].

W Oct 1st	Dick came over and brought in letters 40lbs flour took out sheep.
Sat ,, 4th	Vaughan went to Skokholm. finished the potatoes.
W ,, 15th	Maud Will & Charlie went for a ride
Th ,, 16th	All out shooting.
Tues ,, 21st	Charlie & Walter at the wreck.
Wed ,, 22nd	Charlie & Walter at the wreck.

1885
Th. Jan 15th	Vaughan and I came in. Very rough we landed in the S. Haven.
M ,, 19th	Maudlin. Dick arranged to stay at 3/- per week for ? weeks. Brought surveyors to Midland. 3/- per trip from last Monday. (Probably archaelogists interested in the Celtic huts there—R.H.)
Tues ,, 20th	Dick brought pig in from Hook. Surveyors over.
W ,, 21st	Maud in bed her cold very bad. We made sausages began to smoke the meat.
Sat Feb 7th	Blowing hard but dry—hung up the hams 4 & 1 shoulder 2 chuks. 2 smoked.

M ,, 9th	Vaughan out and my seven little pigs. John Bowen in. Jim came in.
Tues ,, 10th	A wet day killed the pig the last for the season.
F ,, 13th	Sent off a basket to Mrs Lowndes. Mr McKenzie came in to tune the piano.
M ,, 16th	Dick came over they all went to Skokholm to see the ponies.
Th ,, 19th	Blowing fresh. No boat. Hung up 2 Sides 2 hams 1 chuck to smoke.
W Feb 25th	I came to Hermon's Hill. The two girls went to London for their holiday.
F March 6th	I took Bolly for a drive.
W. April 15th	Vaughan drove me home. Harvey drove me to Denant first.
F April 17th	Dick in with barley. (Probably seed—R.H.)
Th ,, 23rd	Old Dick landed beer at the Haven. Did not come up.
Sat May 9th	Dick came over and took them down to Skokholm. Brought back Sailor. Sent out 36lbs Rhubarb.
Th ,, 21st	They all went to Skokholm. Jim went out for the Piebald Pony.
Sat ,, 23rd	Jim came over with the pony and Vaughan and Harvey took them to Skokholm.
M June 1st	Vaughan and the 2 boys went to Skokholm—poor Mory was dead.
Th ,, 4th	Very wet all the men did not know what to do.
Sat ,, 6th	Wool out.
Mon ,, 8th	Vaughan went out to the fair Black sow 6 pigs.
W ,, 10th	Vaughan went to Skokholm with Flora brought Polybody back. The Trewarrens and Harvey went to Dale.
Th ,, 11th	Harry John and Uncle Harry came round from Dale.
F ,, 12th	They all went to Grassholm in Harry's boat.
Sat ,, 13th	We all went to Skokholm in Harry's boat.
M ,, 29th	Butchers in Killed the white bull.
Tues ,, 3oth	Dick out early with the butchers.
W. July 1st	Billy up with letters & bees.
F ,, 3rd	Dick in with the hayrake took out Barley.
F ,, 10th	All in haymaking. Very busy all day. The Miss Summers came in.
Th ,, 16th	Went to Skokholm in the white boat.

"Leading" (carting) hay.

W ,, 22nd	Tom in with a picnic party from Philbeach. The Summers left.
Sat ,, 25th	Vaughan and Dick went to Skokholm. brought Tommy up. took Sailor & Polybody down.
Tues ,, 28th	Vaughan breaking in Tommy. Dick landed clothes & letters. (The washing was sent out to Marloes—R.H.)
W ,, 29th	Blacksmith in. Bolly sent us up a Suin 4½ lbs
Th ,, 30th	Emma Edwards over. took out orders for Hwest
M. Aug. 17th	Jim in did not do the Winch.
Th ,, 27th	A fine day getting on with the harvest.
Fr ,, 28th	busy cutting finished today. Charlie left us & Mabel.
Sat ,, 29th	Busy with the harvest Jim out in the evening
M '' 31st	Dick & Billy over. We settled up everything to Saturday. Commenced the Skokholm work.
Tues Sept 1st	They all went to Skokholm to commence trapping.
W ,, 9th	Blowing and raining no boat could come over to us.
F ,, 11th	Blowing a heavy gale but Dick came up from Skokholm.
1887	(Mrs Davies was away at the beginning of the year.)
Tue April 12th	The little baby was born. Dini doing well.
M May 9th	Baby boy was christened.
Sat ,, 28th	We came home. A fine day.
Sat June 18th	Down to Skokholm with deer. Harry & crew came over.
Tues ,, 21st	Jubilee day.
Th ,, 23rd	Eliza came in.
	(Cash items
	Rec'd 4 Pigs £2-15s
	paid from pigs washing 15s-0
	Mackenzie 10s-0

June 23rd & July 18th
Eliza for 3 weeks & 3 days 10s-6
Nov ,, 1 week & 1 day 3s-6)

M July 18th	Eliza out
W Aug 17th	Churned and made the butter.
M Sept 5th	Vaughan out to the fair. Mr Bonsfield came shot 13 brace.
M ,, 12th	Still fine. Men busy shooting.
F ,, 30th	Dick took sheep down to Skokholm—brought ponies up.
M Oct 3rd	They brought up the traps from Skokholm. Jim out.
Tues '' 4th	Jim in camp on Midland
F ,, 7th	Jim came from Midland. Alice out with the rabbits.

Capt. Vaughan Palmer Davies on a visit to Skokholm with some of his family.
One of the young red deer can be seen on the left.

Sat ,, 8th	Sam & Bowen hired to stay for another year. Out in the evening.
M ,, 17th	Clara & Alice came in early. A fine day.
Tues ,, 18th	Busy putting all things ready.
W ,, 19th	Alice busy packing.
Th ,, 20th	Killed the sheep. 19lbs a quarter.
F ,, 21st	Clara & Alice left. A fine day.
Sun ,, 23rd	We went to Marloes Church.
M ,, 24th	We went to lunch at Butter Hill on to Newton. blowing a gale no boat over.

Tues ,, 25th   Alice's wedding day. A lovely day.
                  We all came home in the evening.
Th '' 27th   Rain all day. We were packing cake all the afternoon.
                  Willie asked me for Maudie.

(They say that one wedding leads to another. Willie was William Singleton Fulshaw, a doctor of Earl Shilton, Leicester—R.H.)

Sat Nov 12th   We came to Denant.
Sun ,, 13th   We went to St Martin's church. N.B. do not go there again.

It would be interesting to know what had prompted Mrs Davies to make such a positive note in her diary not to go to St Martin's church again. It would not seem to have been anything too serious because Maude was married there a few months later, and this will be of interest to some readers. Although, for some unknown reason, Skomer came within the parish of St. Martin's, Haverfordwest, for all practical purposes Marloes was regarded as the parish church.

However, when Alice had married Edward Scriven a couple of weeks before this particular entry, it had been at Llanstadwell parish church. This explains the entry for the day before the wedding, 'We went to lunch at Butter Hill on to Newton.'

Newton, where Vaughan's brother Roch, one of Alice's uncles lived, was a farm on which the Gulf oil refinery has more recently been built, and Alice was married from there.

W Nov 16th   Eliza in.
F ,, 25th   Boat over Eliza out. No rabbits went out today.
Mon Dec 19th No boat over Killed the 2 pigs.
1888
M Jan 2nd   Dick & Billy on day work. Sam and Jenkins came in late. A fine day blowing in the afternoon.
                  (There was then no boat for a week—R.H.)
Sat ,, 7th   Dick & Billy over with letters.
M '' 9th   Vaughan out and the last basket of rabbits. Killed the pig
Tues ,, 10th   A very foggy day. Salted the pig and made sausages.
Tues ,, 17th   Blowing a little from the East no boat over—hung up to smoke 4 hams 3 shoulders 2 jaws.

W ,, 18th	Churned 21 lbs butter.

The ,, 19th   Cold & frosty rain in the evening—finished the cask of beer put it in the Gallon jars (2) no boat over.

F '' 20th   Very foggy. Old Dick over No Maudie. sent out Sam's watch. 73 eggs.

Sat ,, 21st   Thick fog no boat Threshed oats.

M ,, 23rd   Billy Edwards in to kill the pig—Sent out 35 eggs to sell 1½ lbs butter to Katie Jim still out.

Tues ,, 24th   Maudie in—sent out 30lbs butter to E. Edwards for washing which settled the bill.

W ,, 25th   Blowing fresh and foggy. Killed 4 fowls—2 for Myra and 2 for broth
The oat rick blew down. opened the pile of potatoes.

The Feb 2nd   Used 14 eggs Sent out 32—Dick over with Bessy Bowen & Mackenzie. Made pancakes today for all.

Sat ,, 4th   A fine day. Vaughan haltered the colts. Ruby calved.

M ,, 6th   Billy in to kill the pig. Phillis came in. Sent out 56 eggs 4 left in the house, 5 in the hen-house.

Tues ,, 7th   A fine day. The girls weeding in the garden. Salted the pig.

W ,, 8th   Boat over went to Skokholm heard from Harvey— baked bread. Maudie had a lot of presents.

F ,, 10th   Dick & Blacksmith in. Sent out 56 eggs. Maudie & I came to Hook.

Sat ,, 11th
Went to Marloes bought stamps Went to the pillar box Put in to Miss . . .(?) for Parker.

M ,, 13th   Maudie and I came to Hwest snowing all the way. The wedding party arrived at 8.30. Harvey's letter to me came.

Tues ,, 14th   My darling Maudie married. A lovely day— Charlie & Agnes came by morning Mail train.

W ,, 15th   Ada & the gentlemen went off by 11 train—Clara & I Came to Hook blowing too hard to cross over.

The ,, 16th   Clara and I came home—very rough crossing.

F ,, 17th   Put up cake in boxes ready for going away.

Amongst the letters and papers is a receipted invoice for the wedding cake. It was from William Buszard of 197, Oxford Street, London. The 'Bride cake, with extra almond paste was £5-8-6 plus 5s-0d for the packing which was non returnable.' The date of the invoice was Feb 10th, '88 and the receipt 'Paid by chque Feb 21st '88.'

S ,, 18th		Set a hen on 13 eggs.
S ,, 25th		Blowing fresh. Vaughan's cold bad.
1W ,, 29th		Wind went down We were able to come to the dining room very cold no boat.
Th March 1st		Still blowing No boat. had to be up in the sitting room.
M ,, 5th		Richard over for oats. Sent out 64 eggs and orders for Hwest to Ellis Oliver and Greenish. Bluebell calved.
Tues ,, 6th		Bluebell sick. Another fine day. Clara and I went as far as Cot Rock.
W ,, 7th		Richard over for oats had 3 lbs of Pollock up. Set another hen. Hallets oats came in. The Puffins were here today.
F ,, 9th		Old Dick over for oats for Jones Trehill. Paid Vaughan for the rabbits. Vaughan paid for the fish 2/9

The Dining Room.

Seed-time.

Sat ,, 10th	Parker found 11 eggs in hagguard & new shed.
	A fine day put a hen to sit.
	(Haggard is Pembrokeshire for rick-yard—R.H.)
M ,, 12th	A fine day boat over sent out 80 eggs My 2 hens hatched—23 chicks 4 dead in the nest. Maudie sent me some sleeping socks. Lily calved.
F ,, 16th	Hard frost in the morning. Dick in too rough to go to Skokholm and too wild to take Lily out.
M ,, 26th	Vaughan went to Skokholm took down 2 ponies brought 2 more up—Sent out 6lbs butter to Sarah 3 to Billy Edwards. They found an otter.
Tues ,, 27th	Dick over they went to Skokholm brought up 2 ponies Poonah & Flora.
F ,, 30th	Rain in the morning fine afternoon but blowing fresh from N.W. The otter died.
Sat ,, 31st	Boat in took out the 2 white cows and their calves Jim went out with them. Grass seeds in. A fine day.
Sun April 1st	The ducks began to lay.
N ,, 9th	Vaughan out. Sheep in from Hook.
	A fine day. Had the parlour turned out.
Tues ,, 10th	Sent out 10 little pigs to the fair.
	A fine day.
The ,, 12th	We came to Hwest. Clara had her tooth out. We staid at the castle the night.
F ,, 13th	Joe saw me off by train. A lovely day. She went to the Island. I came to Romford got here by 7.00 P.M.

During that holiday Mrs Davies also visited the newly married Maudie at Earl Shilton. A talented girl, Maudie subsequently did the carving on the pulpit at the parish church there.

Tues June 5th	I left Kings Norton and came to Brecon. Charlie met me at the station.
The ,, 7th	Went shopping with Agnes and wet to look at the College.
F ,, 8th	I came to Denant. Ecco met me at the station.
W ,, 13th	Vaughan came in—brought me flowers from Newton.
Tues ,, 19th	Roch out and Twaney. The men in from Hook to cut the hay.
F ,, 22nd	Old Dick very bad.
S ,, 23rd	'A fine day no boat in. Vaughan and Joe went egging.

M ,, 25th	Billy over his father very bad—2 sacks of flour in, one from Shoolbred one from Ellis—brown; Billy Folland came with Billy.
Tues ,, 26th	Men in from Hook & Tre Hill to get in the hay. Old Dick very bad.
W ,, 27th	Billy up his Father a little better.
F ,, 29th	A fine day. Guernsey calved.
Tues July 3rd	A fine day. Maudie and all came in.
W ,, 4th	The Bull went out A cask of oil came in and parcels from Hook.
Th ,, 5th	A lovely day. Harvey better and old Dick much better—sent out two sheepskins.
F ,, 6th	Billy up for milk. Dick much better.
Sat ,, 7th	They all went to Skokholm for the day. had new potatoes and strawberries from Hook.
M ,, 9th	Vaughan went off on his trip. Sent out orders for meal.
Th ,, 12th	Indian corn 120lbs and meal 112lbs. Uncle Tom and Evie came in with Ecco.
F ,, 13th	A lovely day. Will & Maudie went out to see old Dick. Dini came in.
Sat ,, 14th	Maudie and her party all left.
The ,, 19th	Billy took out 2 heifers to Hook.
Fr ,, 27th	Billy came up too rough for him to go back again.
Sat ,, 28th	All left today blowing very fresh.
Tues ,, 31st	Vaughan and Mabel came in.
M Aug 6th	Charlie Agnes and baby came in a fine evening rain in the morning—heard from Harvey.

Perhaps I may be forgiven for a personal note here. Charlie was the first-born son who was brought home as a babe in arms from India round the Cape in the storm. His earlier letters home from Carmarthen were written when he was working there in the Brecon Old Bank. By 1888, however, he had moved to Brecon itself and his mother, when she visited him in June, had visited the College, where his son was to be educated. That son was Percival Valentine Davies, who gave me so much help when I was writing *The Sounds Between*. When he went to Christ College he was taught by the Rev A. E. Donaldson, who was then in the first years of what was to become a great chapter in the school's history. Canon Donaldson was still there in the 1930's and I am one of generations who revere his memory and who consider ourselves privileged to have been taught by him.

Ecco, who is so frequently referred to, was Ethel Fisher of Denant and would seem to have been given her nickname because of her echoing laughter.

Th Aug 9th	The men came in to lead the hay.

(Lead is the Pembrokeshire term for carting hay or corn. Presumably because there would always have been a man at the horse's head leading it by the bridle—R.H.)

F Aug 10th	Mr Say and the Point boys came in—Allie's little boy was born.
The ,, 16th	A very fine day they were cruising all day.
F ,, 17th	Mrs Roch and party came over a lovely day.
S ,, 18th	Meal in. Blacksmith in. Sent out Blossom's colt to Butter Hill.

(Mrs Roch was from Butterhill. Was ther a deal the previous day?—R.H.)

W Aug 22nd	A fine day They went to Skokholm for sheep—We had one killed.
Th ,, 23rd	Blowing very hard sent out the butter for Mrs Williamson and the order for Hwest and the Sheep skin.
M ,, 27th	Billy Folland last trip here, came in with the men from Hook to get in the hay. Eliza in and out.
W '' 29th	Tom Edwards over with Billy—The men went out in the afternoon.
Sat Sept 1st	A fine day Aunt Pye and Ethel came in Eliza went out.
M ,, 3rd	The men went down to Skokholm. Eliza came in. Ned came in.
Tues ,, 4th	Fred Thomson died. Wet all day. No doing anything all day with the corn—cleared off in the evening.
W ,, 5th	Vaughan and Pye went out. Ned out too wet to bind.
Th ,, 6th	A fine day busy binding—Churned in the morning. A sack of Indian corn in Paper from Shoolbred came.
F ,, 7th	Vaughan came in, a fine day, but blowing fresh—found the poullet's nest—busy binding.

Sat ,, 8th   finished binding Charley Hayse (name of a field—R.H.)
                Eliza out settled for all her work in here to today 13/6
                and need butter, for Willie's last years washing 5/-
Tues ,, 11th Boat over with letter and to send bread to Skokholm
                heard from Allie the Baby was christened today.

(The baby was Edward Scriven who told me of the voyage home
round the Cape—R.H.)

Wed ,, 12th   A lovely day Vaughan went out with three ponies—the
                2 girls went out in the white boat.
Tues ,, 18th Busy baking—a lovely day made apple jelly.
W ,, 19th   Vaughan Maudie & Will came in.
Th ,, 20th   Lill & Tom came over. Roch out. Tom recommenced.
                Sent off birds to 4 people—Williamson.Lowndes.
                Fulshaw. Ellis. A basket came fron Aunt Annie.
F ,, 21st   Sent sheep out to Hook. Tom went with them.
M ,, 24th   Charlie came over in the afternoon a lovely day.
Tues ,, 25th Charlie & Will shooting had good sport.
W ,, 26th   Sent off birds
Th ,, 27th   A fine day they were busy shooting.
F ,, 28th   Boat over sent out birds to go off.
                Very wet in the afternoon.
Mon Oct 1st   Charlie and Will out shooting a fine day.
                Maudie busy packing.
Tues ,, 2nd   Uncle Charlie, Maudie and Willie went away.
                A lovely day.
Th ,, 4th   The boat men up on their way to Skokholm.
                blowing fresh.
M ,, 8th   No boat over. The men came up on Sunday and landed
                letters.
Tues ,, 9th   The boat over. Sam and Bowen left us for the fair and
                Sarah went out to go to the fair—the boys left
                altogether.
Th ,, 11th   Boat over with all the things from Skokholm. took
                Pansy out to Hook.
M ,, 15th   Vaughan out to the fair Jim in. took 6 cattle out 3 cows
                3 young ones—Jim set some traps 6 Win(chester—R.H.)
                barly for fowls.
                (Setting inside would be referring to the enclosed land,
                in the centre of the island, as distinct from the rougher

land between the outside boundary walls and the cliffs—R.H.)

Tues Oct 16th   Jim on Midland, Lewis Edwardes came in to go with him. Heard from dear old Harvey he was not so well.

The ,, 18th   Jim still on Midland. A fine day.

F ,, 19th   Sent out the first lot of rabbits from inside and Midland. The traps came from there and Jim commenced outside at Green Plain.

Sat ,, 20th   Boat men over with 6 win(chester)meal from Hook.

M ,, 22nd   Lill & Ecco went away. Clara went with them. Parker out to go to town.

Tues ,, 23rd   Boat men in in the evening with Parker. the Clock back from Munt.

(The old established family firm of Munt had already been in business for nearly a century and are still in business in Haverfordwest—R.H.)

M Oct 29th   Boatmen over for rabbits. No letter from Harvey. Tom Bowen in to thatch.

Tues ,, 30th   Boatmen over and took two yearlings to Hook. Men over in the evening My watch came from Maudie.

Sat Nov 3rd   Boatmen over Tom Bowen out.

M ,, 5th   Stopped the trapping to trim the mangels. Rain in the afternoon.

W ,, 7th   Boat over with blacksmith Sent out 18 eggs to Annie 72 to Hook.

F ,, 9th   Meal in for pigs boatmen in to trim mangolds; My spoon warmer came from Shoolbred. Shut in three pigs to feed.

Tues ,, 13th   A fine day The boat over in the evening George Edwardes came from London. Eliza came in.

W ,, 14th   Finished feathering the ducks and 14 fowls. Rain all day.

Th ,, 15th   Busy packing ducks 26, fowls 12. One packed to go to Annie 4 sent to Hook to Nell.

F ,, 16th   The boat out and Eliza. The Master paid her 1's/4'd so all is settled to date.
Pot of butter to Mrs. Wilkinson.

M ,, 19th   Boat over for rabbits—busy carting mangels.

Tues ,, 20th   Men in all day getting in mangolds.
blowing hard all day.

W ,,	28th	Boat over Lizzie and I went out but only as far as Hook.
The ,,	29th	I went as far as Denant. fine afternoon rain in the morning sent off 17 eggs to Annie.
F ,,	30th	A lovely day we were in Haverford shopping
Sat Dec 1st		I and Lizzie came home from Denant blowing fresh.
Th ,,	6th	Boat over my Sofa and Chair came in. A fine day.
W ,,	12th	Ted, Allie & Vaughan came in. A fine day.
Th ,,	13th	Boat in and meal for pigs—Ted killed 1 Woodcock 1 Snipe 4 Patr—1 Teal 2 Snipe 1 pat from trap.
F ,,	14th	Sent out 18 eggs 4 fowls for market—Ted shot 3 Woodcock 2 Patr
M ,,	17th	Killed the black pig—9sc 16 lbs Churned 24 lbs.
Tues ,,	18th	Rabbits out in the morning Made the puddings Salted the pig.
W ,,	19th	Made sausages and feathered 9 fowls.
The ,,	20th	Killed 2 more fowls. Packed all the parcels and wrote letters Boat over Annie's parcel in flower from Miss Marsh and a picture from the Meas.
F ,,	21st	All the parcels off. rain and wind.
Sat ,,	22nd	Beef in from Mr Davies 46lbs.
M ,,	24th	No boat over rain all day.
Tues ,,	25th	Blowing all day and rain—no boat over.
W ,,	26th	Ted, Allie and baby went out. A fine day. had Maudie's box in and boxes from Arthur and 19 letters.
Th ,,	27th	Fishermen over. Nice all day.
F ,,	28th	Rabbits out sent 39 eggs—8 fowls—a basket for Sophie.

So much for the diaries. And I hope those entries I have selected will have served to show something of the pattern of life on Skomer during the era with which they were concerned.

There are one or two comments which are worth making. There was the entry in the diary to the effect that the Guernsey cow had calved. At that time Guernseys had only very recently been introduced to this country from their native Channel Island, the English Guernsey Cattle Society having been founded as recently as 1884. Renowned for the attractive golden colour and the quality of her milk the Guernsey was regarded very much as the cow of the landed gentry. Note, too, the high standard of the writing in nearly all the letters.

It was also of interest in the correspondence, when Vaughan Davies was taking over from Edward Robinson, to see the reference to Hassel and the inventory. George Hassell was a prominent Haverfordwest auctioneer and estate agent at that time. The fact that he had been engaged would seem to denote a business of some substance.

The request for Vaughan to bring home, if possible, some Malay fowls for Edward Robinson is also of interest. Much reference is made in the letters to the numbers of the poultry and how many chickens they have hatched, but this was the only reference made to their breeding.

However, in his fascinating book *Rings and Rosettes*, Derek Rees, in this valuable history of the Pembrokeshire Agricultural Society, writing of the 1853 show, says, 'At the show there was the rarity of a sale by auction of 'a draft of three dozen pure-bred Cochin-China fowls, the property of Edward Robinson Esq., of Sckomer Island'. Auctioneer Mr George Hassell realised unheard of prices for them.'

So, what with the references to the deer, both on Skomer and Skokholm, to the hares, and the breeding of the poultry and one or two other little items, quite a few things have come to light of which we knew little or nothing previously.

What has not perhaps come through is that Vaughan Davies was a great raconteur and leg-puller, although this has been evident in some of the references it has not been possible to quote. So, as the reference here is to poultry, and as so much of this work is a case of quoting, perhaps I can quote a passage from my book *Caldey* where I was writing about the practice of one of the monks incubating goose eggs under the gulls.

'Murray Mathew, writing in 1894, made some reference to the practice in his book, *The Birds of Pembrokeshire and its islands*. In that instance he was writing of Skomer and referred to an occasion when the farmer on that island, Cat. Vaughan Palmer Davies, told him he had taken the eggs of a carrion crow and replaced them with hens' eggs. The crow hatched them out and,

Capt. Davies, said, the chickens were all black. What the casual reader, all these years later, would not know is that the old retired sea captain was an inveterate leg-puller. Maybe he even saw the enthusiastic old country cleric as the forerunner of the pestiferous band of professional countrymen destined to proliferate in the years to come. If he also fostered some fond notion of discouraging the proliferation universally of environmentalists, conservationists, ecologists and all the other species of that current growth industry, he fostered it, like the incubating crows and gulls, in vain.'

Lastly, it must be worth a mention that Mrs Davies's little diaries were The Lady's Universal Pocket Diary. The first pages were given over to pictures and stories and little poems and thoughts apposite to the times.

In the diary for 1887 a certain Mrs Ellis offers 'Advice to Wives.'

'How to Welcome A Tired Husband

I Had not finished my solitary meal before my husband came, looking jaded and worn, and withal, as I thought, a little out of temper. What could be the matter? it was on my lips to ask; but I fortunately checked the words before they passed further. Nothing annoys a man more than to be eagerly questioned when he comes home tired. Give him a neatly-served dinner, or a pair of easy slippers and a cup of tea and let him eat and drink in peace, and in time he will tell you of his own proper motion, all you wish to know. But if you begin the attack too soon the chances are that you will be rewarded by curtly-spoken monosyllables.

Man's Love.

It must ever be borne in mind that man's love, even in its happiest exercise, is not like woman's; for while she employs herself through every hour in fondly weaving the beloved image into all her thoughts, he gives to her comparatively few of his; and of these, perhaps, not the loftiest or the best.

It is a wise beginning, then, for every married woman to make her mind to have many rivals in her husband's attentions, though not in his love; and among these, I refer to the journal or newspaper of the day, of whose absorbing interest some wives are weak enough to evince a sort of childish jealously, when they ought rather to congratulate themselves that their most formidable rival is one of paper.'

No doubt to have dared even to quote such thoughts will have been to put me irretrievably beyond the pale as far as the liberated ladies of today are concerened. I have no regrets, however, and make no apologies.

To those who would build a happy marriage the words still hold much of wisdom. And they were written in an age when family was important and when marriages were made to last. To have been privileged to read through the letters and diaries of such good people is to be reminded of so much which was worthwhile about old-fashioned values.

How much will our own letters and diaries tell those who come after us a century and more from now? Or shall we only bequeath them video tapes?

A Sea Shanty

Fifty years ago the Brython Press published a book *Cerddi Portinllaen* (1936) by J. Glyn Davies. One of the old sea shanties it included was *Heibio Ynys Sgogwm*.

> Heibio Ynys Sgogwm: O ai o!
> Llong yn hwy-lio'n hwyn-drwm: O ai o!
>
> Heibio Ynys Sgogwm: O ai o!
> Llong yn mynd fel stemar.
>
> Dal i'r de-orllewin;
> Adre bob yn dipyn.
>
> Tacio'n ol, i'r gogledd;
> Adre'n syth o'r diwedd.
>
> Cwrs am Ynys Enlli;
> Hwylio'n syth am dani.
>
> Heibio 'Nysoedd Gwylan;
> Llanw'n mynd ar garlam.

Hwylio drwy Swnt Enlli;
Llanw'n mynd fel cenlli.

Gwynt yn deg am G'narfon;
Wedi morio digon.

PASSING SKOKHOLM ISLAND

Passing Skokholm Island; O ai o!
Sailing late, heavy laden: O ai o!

Passing Skomer Island;
Ship going like a steamer;

Heading to South-West;
Home before long

Tacking back to North;
Home quick at last

Course for Bardsey Island;
Sailing straight towards her

Passing seagull islands;
Tide racing along

Sailing through Bardsey Island;
Tide like a torrent

Wind fair for Caernarfon;
Been sailing enough.

I felt that this shanty was worth mentioning for more than one reason. In the first place, it tells something of the routes the old sailing ships would have taken.

Clearly, North Wales sailing vessels of any size, coming up round Linney Head, would not be the most suitable craft for taking up through Jack Sound or Ramsey Sound at certain states of wind and tide, and their skippers would no doubt have deemed

6

Heibio Ynys Sgogwm

Heibio Ynys Sgomar ; *O ai o !*
Llong yn mynd fel stemar : *O ai o !*

Dal i'r de-orllewin ;
Adre bob yn dipyn.

Tacio'n ol i'r gogledd ;
Adre'n syth o'r diwedd.

Cwrs am Ynys Enlli ;
Hwylio'n syth am dani.

Heibio 'Nysoedd Gwylan ;
Llanw'n mynd ar garlam.

Hwylio drwy Swnt Enlli ;
Llanw'n mynd fel cenlli.

Gwynt yn deg am G'narfon,
Wedi morio digon.

CERDDI PORTINLLAEN.

18

it expedient to avoid such hazards as far as possible. Having left Skokholm, and then Skomer on their starboard quarter, they would have avoided, not only Ramsey, but the even more dreaded Bishops and Clerks. Hence the 'De-orllewin', a long tack out on a sou'-west course. Then comes the 'tacio'n ol . . .' to put about on the home tack to Bardsey Sound on one long reach. So there was no mention of Ramsey.

The other point of interest is that, when these hard-bitten crews were sailing these waters and singing their shanties, both Skomer and Skokholm were being farmed by men who had themselves 'been all over.' Whilst Capt. Vaughan Palmer Davies was on Skomer, for a good part of that time Skokholm was being farmed by Capt. Henry Edward Harrison, and it was shortly after his death, in 1881, that Capt. Davies rented Skokholm also.

Not long before he died, in his nineties, I spent some hours with the late Tommy Harrison, Capt. Harrison's 'natural' grandson. Truly he was one of life's characters, and it was a meeting I shall never forget. I had been forewarned what to expect because he had, apparently, been to the doctor some years previously for maybe the first time in his life. He was at last, however, having some trouble with his leg and, eventually, the doctor said, 'How old are you, Mr Harrison?'

'Eighty-four,' replied Tommy.

'My goodnesss! Eighty four! You must remember you've had that old leg a long time.'

'I knows that,' said Tommy. 'But I've had th'other bugger just as long and there's nothing wrong with him.'

He did not disappoint me when I eventually met him, and he gave me a great deal of useful information as I have already related in *The Sounds Between*. He was, however, extremely deaf and it was a long row to hoe. His opening gambit, when the word Skokholm eventually registered with him, was to demand, 'What do you think of all these convicts escaping all over the place then, master? How don't they put 'em out on Skokholm Island, that's what I'd like to know? The buggers would never come from there. No, never.' Pembrokeshire people invariably say how instead of why.

I had to admit he had a good point, and from there on we got on famously. I knew something of his lineage, and approached the subject tactfully and courteously. He only chuckled, however, and said, 'I never had no father, Master. I was washed up by the tide!'

And the twinkle in his eyes, and the smile on his wrinkled old face, told exactly how much he cared what the world thought about it. He was one of the many of the island people who had been born in one of the cottages at Martinshaven.

For my own part I can only say I shall always feel privileged to have spent time with so many such marvellous characters.

Chapter 2

Random Writings

The whole point and purpose of my writing *Cliffs of Freedom* was
to tell the story of Reuben Codd and his connection with Skomer.
In doing it certain facts had to be stated, so there was considerable criticism of the West Wales Field Society as constituted and
operating at that time. That meant criticism of their bird-ringing
and seal-ringing activities and quite a few other activities as well,
including their antics with the Soay sheep.

Within a week or so of publication, on November 24th 1961 to
be precise, a report appeared in the *Western Mail* saying,
'Members of the West Wales Field Society yesterday replied to
statements made by farmer-journalist Roscoe Howells in his book
Cliffs of Freedom, published this week and reviewed by Westgate
in yesterday's *Western Mail*.'

The hon. secretary at that time was a Mr D. Miles, and he was
quoted as saying, 'The society will have to consider what action
to take in view of Mr Howells's unfounded allegations, and therefore I do not wish to make any comment at this stage.'

I am old enough to know that memory plays funny tricks and
now, a quarter of a century later, I cannot for the life of me
remember how many nights sleep, if any, I would have lost over
such a hideous threat. What action would they take indeed?
Would they come and put some of their rings on me? When would
they strike?

I could be wrong, of course, but I do not recall losing any sleep
at all. The chances are I could have been highly amused, the same
as a good many other people were. Anyway, we waited in vain.
No further announcement was made and no action was taken.

A year or so afterwards, at some public lunch or other, I sat next
to a man who was one of the sycophantic members of the Council
of that Society at the time, and he told me that he disagreed with
the views I had expressed in my book. But he couldn't tell me

which ones they were, and then, under further questioning, it transpired that he had not actually read the book. Have you ever tried discussing anything intelligently with people like that?

More recently, by way of interest, I had a look at the old minutes of that Society and was disappointed to find that there was no record of anything having been discussed. Not that that signifies, because the minutes are to sketchy, and there is such a paucity of information, that they are as near worthless to posterity as anything could be. I know one thing for sure. I was Honorary Clerk to a Parish Council for ten years and, if the minutes I left as a record of the various discussions had not been of ten times more use than this lot I would consider the parishioners to have been ill served indeed.

One thing about which I felt strongly was the way migratory birds had been tormented in what had become known on Skomer as the Invasion of 1946 when Walter Sturt had rather ill-advisedly let the island to the Society for a season. Fears were rife in 1959 that the same thing was about to start happening all over again now that the Society had acquired control of Skomer, and most of my criticism was on that count. To show myself as a fair-minded sort of character I referred to the bird-ringing currently being done on neighbouring Skokholm as being within the realms of sanity. My personal knowledge of Skokholm at that time was slight and, over that particular reference, I was quietly taken to task by the Welsh teacher and author, the late Roy Saunders, who had known the islands for many years. In a letter he wrote to me at the time he said,

'If you want to write on anything that deserves censure why not have a crack at the Skokholm bird ringers who collect a sackful of auks to take them for ringing & recording at their convenience during which time the herring gulls & black backs make whoopee over the unguarded eggs which cannot of course be repeated during that season. Believe me Roscoe, a few days on Skokholm with a camera could produce a tale that would shake the bird world.

Their claim on Skokholm is that they ring greater numbers each year. The mass turn-out to hound rare visiting birds into the traps applies far more on Skokholm than on Skomer where it would be more or less impossible owing to Skomer's size and roughness.'

Much has been written over the years about Skokholm being Britain's first bird observatory, but few know much about the other side of the coin.

There are, however, a few vague references in those old minutes which ring a bell and lead me to think I was not exactly the Society's Number one pin-up. Eventually, as a result of pressure from here and there and one and another, their seal-ringing had to stop, and when they had a new lease on Skokholm the bird-ringing there had to stop, and the Soay sheep had to be disposed of and, oh dear me, there was some upheaval altogether. But the only personal reference to me was in a minute of Sept 22nd 1962 under the heading, 'Honorary Warden's Report.

'*Welsh Farm News*'

'An article published in *Welsh Farm News* by Brock had led to correspondence being received from members who considered the article offensive!'

Offensive indeed. There'd be a thing, as the saying goes, if anybody ever read that minute and took any notice of it.

Ben Brock was the pen-name under which I contributed a piece every week to *Welsh Farm News*, subsequently *Farm News*, subsequently defunct. Happy days.

Of course, after all these years, I had no idea what the article could have been because I knew I had on odd occasions made passing reference to what was happening on the islands., Sometimes the column was serious, occasionally sad, sometimes humorous and happy nonsense, and sometimes just plain, old-fashioned stirring things up a bit. So, not remembering into which of these categories, if any, the offending article had fallen, I looked it up. It appeared on August 18th, 1962, and you must judge for yourselves how offensive it was.

'I hope you will not read this column this week as it is nothing but a great deal of foolishness about something very nebulous which, as I have explained to you before, means without foundation.

I am thus prompted by a headline in a national paper this week which screamed to the world—'grey-rumped sandpiper is a phoney.'

The report then went on to state that some character, who once lived in Sussex, was supposed to have come across a lot of rare birds in that area, but it now looks as if he had them brought into the country on ice from the foreign parts where they used to flit about a bit and whistle ye merry tune.

As this character has now been dead for about twenty years, however, I do not suppose he minds very much what they say about him and I'll bet he had a good old laugh in his time. You will understand from what I have previously told you that these birdy types are very serious indeed with their rings and measurements and what not. Certainly they will be much disturbed to learn that the grey-rumped sandpiper and many other such rarities are nothing but the old phonus bolonus.

Furthermore I know something about the old phonus bolonus myself and have likewise written little pieces for you at odd times about all such odd birds as the mugwump, the elephant bird, the mustard bird and, of course, the oozlum bird.

I am very interested in this most recent case of the old phonus bolonus, however, as I think it might explain something that has been troubling some of us in these parts for a good many years.

Once upon a time there was a character writing a few pieces about this and that round the islands of West Wales to try to earn a crust, and he also wrote down in his book each day about the birds which were all round and about the place. He also gave instructions to the trapper, who was catching rabbits on the island, and also the two lads who were helping the trapper, to take note of all creatures unusual so that he could record all facts about them in his book.

Well, on this occasion, Master had gone away in the boat to take the rabbits to the mainland and he was gone for a day and a night and returned late in the afternoon on the following day. So after they have eaten their supper Master gets out his book to write down what you might call the vital statistics and he says 'Now,' he says, 'what is there to report and what do you see whilst I am away?'

So the trapper takes his pipe out of his mouth and spits in the fire till the bars sizzle more than somewhat and he says, 'Well there's nothing very much to report except about the little bord.' You must also understand that such characters as I am referring to pronounce it 'bord' although you and I who have had the benefit of this here education would call it 'bird.'

So Master pricks up his ears and says very excited, 'What bird was this? What bird?'

So the trapper says, 'Oh 'twas a pretty little bord. Had a bit of red on her head and blue down her belly and all green under her wings with all yellow spots and a lot of white and her tail was . . .'

'Yes,' says Master sharpish, 'where was it?'

'Well I tell you now,' says the trapper, 'I'd pulled up the traps down south side and I thinks to myself it's hardly worth setting these again now with Master being off in case the weather comes up rough and he don't come back with the boat so off I goes to have a look at the traps over beyond the old well. An that's when I seen the little bord.'

'Where was she?' says Master.

'Why,' says the trapper, 'there she was in the trap. And oh she was a pretty little bord. She had a bit of red on her head and blue down her . . .''

'Yes, all right,' says Master getting a bit curly because of the slow way the story is being told, 'where is the bird now?'

'Well that's what I'm trying to tell you,' says the trapper. 'I could see she was dead of course, so . . .'

'Well if she was dead,' shouts Master, getting very worked up indeed, 'where is she now? Let me see her at once.'

So the trapper takes his pipe put of his mouth and has another spit which goes right between the fire bars this time and then he says, 'Now that is what I am trying to tell you, but I don't see how I can tell you if you're going to keep on interrupting.'

So Master bites his lip and tries very hard to stay quiet and be patient. So the trapper starts off again, 'So like I told you I'd pulled up the traps down south side and I thinks to myself it's hardly worth setting 'em. Well I told you what I thought like so I went over to the traps beyond the old well and there was the little bord in the trap.'

So the trapper looks at Master, but Master is obviously listening patiently and is showing no sign of interrupting again, so the trapper goes on to describe the bird again and in fact adds a few more colours and spots and stripes which he doesn't think of the first time.

'So now then,' says the trapper, 'I thinks to myself Master will surely want to see this little bord because I knows how you likes writing down all about the little bords in the book every night. So I takes her out of the trap and puts her in my pocket for you to see her.'

'Well now then,' says Master between his teeth, 'let me see her.'

'That's just it,' says the trapper, 'I haven't got her.'

'Haven't got her,' screamed Master, 'then where is she?'

'Well it's like I said,' says the trapper. 'I knowed you'd want to see her so I put her up there on the mantlepiece. And, oh, she was a pretty little bord. A bit of red on her head and blue. . .'

'Where is she now?' wails Master with fire in his eyes and his mouth open and dribble running down his chin. 'Where is she now?'

'Well that's like I said, ' says the trapper, 'I put her there on the mantlepiece for I knowed you'd want to see her and there she was last night when we went to bed. But she was gone this morning.'

'Gone,' raves Master. 'How could she go if she was dead!'

'Ah,' says the trapper, 'the little mice must have had her.'

Foolish this column may be. Yes, and many other of the adjectives you might see fit to apply to it. But we have never yet given it over to obscenity. So I can't really tell you of the oaths which shattered the island night.

Maybe it doesn't matter very much, but it's odd how the thought comes back after all these years.

In fact it is beginning to look as if the trapper was no better than some of these birdy types and I'm thinking his bird must go into the record books with the grey-rumped sandpiper and all that lot.

If you ask me his bird was nothing but the old phonus bolonus.'

I wouldn't call any of that offensive exactly, but there it is, there's no accounting for taste. A few years before that I had written one or two other little pieces.

As far as I was concerned my days of roaming carefree on Skomer were over and done with. To have been there in Reuben's time was something special and nothing could ever be the same again.

In June of 1959 I stayed with Reuben at Martinshaven and wrote a few lines on that occasion. Brinley Hooper, Reuben's nephew, had taken on the contract to build the new cedar wood house on the island and, in the event, I stayed over there for a few nights. If anybody asked any questions I was driving the tractor for him. Then, in the October, with the house nearing completion, I went over for a week and had a riotous time. Whenever conversation palled around the fire of an evening Brinley would demand that I should recite Robert Service's *Cremation of Sam McGee*. Two Ben Brocks reported progress, and I quote herewith the one for October 31st, 1959.

The new house nearing completion on Skomer.

'When I took my leave for what I, at any rate, am convinced was a hard-earned holiday, I thought that maybe you could manage for a week or so without my erudite observations on matters agricultural.

The thought occurs, however, that rather than see a blank in the usual corner, and matters agricultural being out of the question at the moment, you might in lieu of, like to know how things are shaping on this fair island. For, if you read last week's edition, you will remember that I was bound for Skomer.

Dark and stormy waters delayed the crossing for twenty four hours, but now I'm here. And there's an outside chance that arrangements might be made for these lines to reach the editor's desk so that you will be able to keep yourselves up-to-date.

And, believe me, friends, you've got a finger in this pie. Whether you like it or not. But we'll come to that bit later.

First of all I should tell you that, on arrival, I discovered that those who might now be regarded as residents and who have reverted to something little better than half-savage, had refused to put the clock back.

Rather like the artistic type who handed in his day return ticket at the barrier and, on having it pointed out to him that it was nearly a year out-dated explained to the inspector that time mattered not to him.

So then, with these people. And, in view of my never-ending campaign against this iniquity, that propably makes you laugh your eye out. But it does serve to emphasise the sense of leaving the thing alone all the year round.

It merely means that, unlike the sailor who got up with the lark and went to bed with the wren we get up with the lark and go to bed with the gulls.

In between times everything else is an hour earlier than with the rest of the country. We are occasionally reminded of this because, in the way the old-time traders undermined the way of life of the Red Indians, some rotten white man flogged a portable radio to these poor innocents. Such is the extent of our depravity.

When this miserable box isn't churning out the worst that radio Luxembourg can offer it gets switched on to the news and then immediately turned off because nobody wants to be that miserable.

So that, for the most part, it's a case of forgotten by the world and by the world forgot.

But I wouldn't like you to forget about the wonderful bungalow which you taxpayers, via the Nature Conservancy, have almost finished building here. It sure is some shack, friends. It was so important to stick it in the right place that, in order to counteract the fearful slope, sufficient concrete blocks went into the foundation to build a cavity-walled bungalow of the same size on any flat part of the island. When you realise that there are at least 400 acres of dead flat land on which to build you will see how important it was to have it where it is.

These blocks were imported after the fearful row which followed exposure of the fact that the foundations were supposed to be of the stones which would have to be torn from the old farm walls where the Manx shearwaters make their nests.

In this three-bedroomed bungalow there are kitchen sinks various, one bath and three W.C.s. So that there shall be no room for doubt let me explain that this abbreviation stands for water closet. And there are three of them.

The fact that the joint has been stuck near the well which in anything like a dry season won't provide enough water to keep even one of the said closets going is the concern and misfortune of those who won't be able to use them. [I am happy to report that this gloomy forecast turned out to be incorrect. R.H.]

Light is to be provided by liquid gas with a patent name. In addition to two geysers and one cooker there are to be no fewer than 34 (thirty four) lights! There are other items, friends. But don't let me bore you.

Small wonder that you taxpayers are now running out of cash and it has been decided, for example, that you can't afford a decent grate for the lounge. Instead you have had to settle for a ye olde worlde effort made of pebbles from the beach. Odds and ends of items that would cost another copper or two are now strictly taboo. The economy drive is on. So rejoice ye taxpayers and be of glad heart.

As to the future, there are already signs that the Skomer voles are in for a high old time tearing up the insulation board which lines this wonderful cedar-wood bungalow. But you taxpayers refused to settle for spending half as much money to do up the old farm-house. Stones and slates weren't good enough. So on your own heads be it.

By candle light conference the other night we decided that if you could see the head boss struggling to get a tractor up a gradient of 1 in 3 you'd decide he was crackers. He said he decided he was crackers long ago after he could see what he's taken on by coming here at all.

Last time I was hereabouts I wrote a little piece for you about the experiment of crossing Welsh Mountain ewes with Soay ewes. You might as well call the latter goats and be done with. You'd be much nearer the mark.

I think I explained to you last week that the experiment has already been accounted a failure. The Welsh Mountain ewes have all been recaptured and removed. All bar one.

She, poor lonely soul, is still chasing the Soays round the rocky perimeter of this 700-acre stronghold.

After the drought and shortage of grass you can take my word for it that she is now in superb racing condition. And then some.

Maybe I'll open a book so that my most excellent companions can state their case as to what they think might happen if she ever does catch up with them.

Maybe, of course, they're all just dashing for the blade of grass they thought they saw about to grow. For everything is now so bare that one evening a rabbit was actually seen on top of a clump of brambles where he had climbed in search of some green leaf.

One of my old masters at school used to say that a phenomenon was a cow sitting on a thistle. He just didn't know a thing, of course. And his false teeth were loose anyway, so we were inclined to laugh about him.

You will know from all this that I am well-content with my humble portion here below. I lack for nothing. I don't even have to open my own tins as in days of yore.

In preparation for this screed I said to the most estimable, blue-eyed colleen, a true daughter of owld Oireland, who ministers to our every need, 'And what shall I be after sayin' about you, my darlint?'

To which she replied, 'Say not'ting at all as long as it's the trut'.'

Yes indeed, 'Say nothing at all as long as it's the truth.' Not a bad motto I'm after thinking. And, so help me, every word of what I've written is true enough. It also explains about the Irish.

And so, to the strains of Tommy Steele shouting his guts out on Radio Luxembourg, I bid you good-day.

I'll be back bye and bye. Worst luck.'

What I did not write about at that time was Brinley and the cock pheasants. There had been pheasants on Skomer since Vaughan Davies's time, but for some years there had been no control over them, for there had been little or no shooting, and the cocks had become predominant. Reuben, who knew every inch of the island, and just about everything that moved there, was quite certain that no pheasants had reared any young on Skomer for a few years.

Probably the ideal ratio with pheasants would be one cock bird to about five or six hens. Where there are too many cocks they will fight over a hen on the nest, so that the eggs will be smashed, or the young ones killed or deserted. The hen pheasant is a notoriously poor mother at the best of times. During one of our interminable candle-light discussions Brinley and I decided that, if the pheasants were to continue to breed on Skomer, something needed to be done. He was due to hand over the house on completion fairly soon and we knew that, under the new regime, nothing as sensible as shooting the cocks would be undertaken. Somebody might try to put some rings on them, but that would have been about the height of their aspirations and the sum total of their ideas on conservation.

The following day was devoted to conservation and Brinley shot six cock pheasants. A deadly shot, he dropped every one with the first barrel, and the only hen to rise flew free. All the cocks had spurs on them that would have done credit to a cavalry officer.

There were then only two or three hens there, but they now began to breed again.

At that time, as well as farming a hundred acres with a dairy herd, a flock of sheep and growing some corn, I was also working full-time for a weekly paper. So, when the occasional chance came for a break, I needed to take it and, in the summer of 1960, I went to Skokholm for a week. I quite enjoyed it, and there was some good company there, but it was not the sort of thing about which I could become enthusiastic. Sleep was just about as much as I wanted to do.

Ben Brock duly reported on August 6th, 1960

'I told you I was going on holiday, didn't I, and here I am. Though when or whether you will ever read this is anybody's guess, and dependent on the weather, and whether a boat ever passes this way.

Skokholm 1960.

For you know where I go when the spirit moves. It's over the waves to the islands. And this time it's Skokholm. Further out than Skomer and even less accessible.

But there are people here. Creatures of odd habits, I find, but they have their uses. They cook for example and help with the washing up and everybody mucks in together and, taking it in turns, we pump away to get water from the well to the tank, which is all frightfully jolly.

In any case there are only a dozen of us, so that the washing up and pumping doesn't really amount to very much.

There is also a lighthouse with three friendly keepers who are glad to see just anybody from the outside world.

One, upon being asked why he became a lighthouse keeper, said, it was because he isn't right in the head. I don't believe this, however. They all seem quite all right to me. One is so browned off that he is just waiting for the day when he comes up on the pools so that he can go and buy a lighthouse of his own. Which just goes to show you.

In between times, whilst we are not washing up and pumping water, we watch birds and that, and everybody puts rings on their legs (the birds' legs), and they all make a lot of notes in books. I don't think you'd be very interested in this.

But there is one little point I felt I ought to tell you about.

It's about the Soay sheep. You'll die laughing.

For you remember before I set off I told you about what happened to the thirty odd Soay sheep on eighteen acres St. Margaret's Island who got struck by lightning before they could get down to eat the seaweed like they used to do two thousand years ago.

Well there were some Soays on Skokholm. About seventy or so. But, although the island is over two hundred acres, it was decided last autumn to get rid of them because it was so bare there would not be enough for them to last the winter. Especially if they couldn't get down to the seaweed!

And, of course, they might not get struck by lightning the same as those on St. Margaret's which would very conveniently put them out of their suffering.

So everybody went out on a battue and shot about sixty Soays, leaving a dozen.

During the winter ten of these died, but I don't know why, and then there were two.

These two are still here. And they are ewes. Which leads me to the point of the story.

When I wrote to you from Skomer last year about the experiment of crossing Welsh mountain ewes with Soay ewes, I told you that these creatures looked more like goats.

Certainly none of the other sheep ever met up with the Soays and they just wouldn't have any truck with them.

But out here it's different. For we have some goats. They don't belong to anybody, but they're here.

They don't belong to the lighthouse anyway. And they don't belong to us. But it seems they were left here by 'the bird people' sometime.

Once upon a time there was a billy goat and there was a nanny.

This island is three miles from the land and it is very pleasant here. I should imagine, though, that time could hang very heavy on your hands, especially in winter if you were such a silly old goat that you didn't have much interest in birds, and when the birds have all gone away anyway.

So now there is also a young goat here and that makes three. As luck would have it he's a young billy. And that's going to complicate things.

But like I was saying about these Soays. I said before, they looked like goats. And the proof of the sheep is in the mating.

I'm not sticking my neck out. Not saying anything at all.

I'm just lying on the cliff catching up on some sleep to which I am very partial and now and again keeping an eye on the sheep and goats and things in general.

And the Soays and the goats have palled up. Yes, but definitely something more than just good friends. They graze maybe ten yards apart.

But I know about goats. And I've seen this dirty great billy goat with a long beard, and a wicked look in his eye and I'll wager I know what he's thinking. And my betting is that if these Soays aren't a good bit more careful than they're being just at the moment they're going to miss the last 'bus home one dark night just when they're least expecting it.

Especially with the youngster also just beginning to sit up and take notice.

If ever that should happen I'd like to come out here again to report back. But there's a dead keen birdwatcher here who has just left school and is going to start going to college to learn to be a vet. He's going to spend six years learning to be a vet. I've spent all my life thinking about sheep and billy goats and the birds and the bees and that.

I have been propounding my views, and this boyo says that it won't happen and, even if it does, nothing will happen because of Jean's and I said what the hell did Jean have to do with it? It's this dirty great Billy is the one to watch.

And you know and I know that I know what I'm talking about.'

In the evenings, over a cup of cocoa and a biscuit, everybody had to report what birds had been sighted during the day, together with a description of anything unusual or of particular interest, and the warden would write down details in a book. I didn't have the nerve to think of anything as colourful as the one of which I was to write a couple of years later and be accused of being offensive, but some of them saw quite a few birds of great interest. The book became known as the 'daily liar.'

My own contribution was to write a few lines in the visitors' book and I am grateful to the present incumbents for making it available to be quoted here.

From the Skokholm visitors' book, July 1960

'Hiawatha's Puffin Ringing

You shall hear how Hiawatha
Came to ring the little puffins
Came to see the gulls and gannets
Hook the birds upon the ledges
Chase them all into the big traps
Listen to the manx shearwaters;

How he crossed the stormy water
Through the wild waves madly tossing
Clutching tightly to his camera
To his glasses and his bird-book,
Thus did joyful Hiawatha
Come to Skokholm in the summer
With his brave heart wildly beating
Thus he came to ring the puffins.
　　There he gazed upon the homestead
Gazed upon the mighty cliff tops
Gazed upon the noble lighthouse
Gazed upon the birds a-flying
Gazed upon the great waves breaking
Gazed in wonder all about him;
Saw the pots and pans and dishes
Saw the rules and regulations
Learned to live with other people
And potatoes how to peel them.
Learned to prime the pump with water
And the handle how to work it.
　　Thus did weary Hiawatha
Steal away into a corner
There to rest and idly slumber
Pass the time in idle slumber.
Thus to feed him and revive him
With the rarest fragrant spices
Came the faithful Minnehaha,
Laughing water, brown-eyed Margaret,
　　Then did Hiawatha bravely
Take himself unto the big chief
To the Warden in his wigwam
In his wigwam sat the Warden;
Hiawatha spake unto him
And he told a wond'rous story
How he'd crossed the stormy water
Clutching tightly to his camera
To his glasses and his bird-book
With his brave heart wildly beating
How he'd come to ring the puffins
How he'd eaten how he'd slumbered
How his strength returned unto him.

Then the Warden in his wigwam
Lit his pipe and puffed it slowly
Gazed on Hiawatha sadly
Ere he spake unto him this wise:
　'See the wild stretch on the cliff top
Where the fern is growing thickest
When the birds that passed in springtime
Shall return when comes the autumn
In the fern they will deceive us
There they'll hide and we'll not find them.
But there is a scythe and whetstone
Bent the blade and handle broken,
Take them, oh, my Hiawatha,
Gird thy loins and heave thy shoulders
Bend thy back, compress thy belly,
And thy mighty shoulders heaving
With thy scythe so wildly swinging
Clear the wild stretch on the cliff top.'.
　Thus did lonely Hiawatha
Heaving with his mighty shoulders
Swinging with the scythe so wildly
Bent the blade and handle broken
Slay the fern upon the cliff top
Till the sweat was rolling off him
Till his shirt was clinging to him
Till the gnawing at his vitals
Told him that he was black starving
Made him look where flew the meal flag
Listen where the bell was ringing
Hasten back unto the wigwam
There to find his Minnehaha
Slapping food before the paleface:
Ravenous he ate his kipper.
　Passed the time for Hiawatha
Food and sleep, and sleep and labour:
But when none was there to stay him
Passed the time in idle slumber,
Till at last across the water
They beheld the spray was flying
And they knew the boat was coming:
Thus did Hiawatha sadly
With the rest go frantic dashing

Thus departing from the island
Clutching tightly to his camera
To his glasses and his bird book.
Thus departed Hiawatha,
But he hadn't ringed a puffin.

July 1960.'

To revert for a moment to the minutes of the old West Wales
Naturalists' Trust, as it became, there is a bare, brief entry for July
26th, 1963. 'Mr Ben R. Feaver was appointed chairman for the
ensuing year.'

There is no mention of any background involving the change,
or to any votes of no confidence, and no recording of appreciation
or even as much as a vote of thanks to the outgoing chairman. But
then, life is like that.

The following year, as a result of this change at the top, I went
again to Skomer where a new warden, David Saunders, and his
wife, Shirley, had taken over. They seemed a nice enough young
couple, but eyed me with some suspicion, or so I thought. I was
staying in one of 'Reuben's chalets' up at the old farm buildings.

By about the third day they must have come to the conclusion
that I was at least civilised, for Shirley asked me if I would like to
come down the following evening to 'have it out.' My book. All
the dreadful things I had been writing and saying.

So I went down to the new house the following evening, we
talked until after one o'clock in the morning, and we have been
good friends ever since. They were keen and seemed quite
knowledgeable. But when it came to the politics of the business,
and all the background chicanery, they were just a pair of blue-
eyed innocents. And that was the aspect, of course, which had
disturbed so many people. I like to think that I enlightened them
somewhat and that it served them in good stead as the years went
by.

I made no secret of the fact that my only interest in joining the
West Wales Field Society was to try to help to protect Skomer
from the Society itself. I became one of the enemies within. The
Trust, as it now functions, owes an untold debt of gratitude to

such people as John Barrett, the late Tommy Warren Davies, who was a relation of Vaughan Palmer Davies, and to dear old Reuben himself, for being willing to stir the muddy waters before the stream ran clear.

When the time came to remove the secretary I was more than happy to go along to the A.G.M. in the spring of 1976 and speak in support of David Saunders. In due course he became administration/conservation officer and, more recently, Director. Nobody is happier than I am to be able to say that the Trust prospers, does a good job of work, and is served on a voluntary basis by some splendid people.

In 1985, one of them, Jack Donovan, was awarded the Idris Davies Memorial Trust Trophy by the county branch of the National Farmers' Union for services to agriculture. It was largely in recognition of his efforts to help to maintain a sensible balance between farming and conservation, and was immensely popular.

As these lines are being written it has just been announced that Stephen Sutcliffe, another who has given years of voluntary service to the Trust, has taken on the job of warden on Skomer in succession to Mike Alexander, who did a good job of work in that capacity for ten years.

The evening I called on David and Shirley Saunders was June 24th, 1964. Those who are interested in such matters as Halley's Comet could probably tell you that there was a total eclipse of the moon that night. I shall never forget it, for it answered one question for me unequivocally.

There are people who will tell you that shearwaters only come to land during dark nights. Others reckon that they come to land every night, but that it is only on dark nights that they need to call in order to get their bearings from their mates. In the small hours of the morning, as I walked back from the Saunders' house, the place was as silent as the tomb. Then came the eclipse, pitch darkness and, within minutes, the cacophony was unbelievable, as if all the fiends in hell had been let loose. As the eclipse passed, it was all over, and the island sank back to sleep and to a great silence.

Stephen and Anna Sutcliffe.
Pic. Western Telegraph.

Don't ask me why, but I stayed up until four o'clock reading Howard Spring. And then, as Robert Drane had written of a similar experience on Skomer so long ago, 'I went to bed feeling I had seen the world of shades, and when I come to stand at the dark river's side I shall feel that I have been somewhere thereabouts before.'

Chapter 3

More Letters

I mentioned in *The Sounds Between* that, when reports appear in the papers concerning the islands, there is often some confusion between Skomer and Skokholm, and that neither do some mainland dwellers know the difference between them. There was an interesting example of this half-a-century ago. I had been aware of the little local difficulty, as I believe such affairs are called, but I did not come across the correspondence until recently.

'Western Telegraph, May 21st, 1936
Roose Sessions
A NOVELIST'S DOG

Ronald Mathias Lockley, The Novelist, of Martin's Haven, Marloes, described as a farmer, was summoned for a like offence.

P.C. Priest said that Mrs Lockley told him her husband, who was then in London, had not applied for an exemption.

Supt. C.B. James: Did she suggest the dog was under six months?

The Constable: No. He added it appeared to be a full grown dog.

In a letter from Skomer Island, Mr Lockley explained that he had writen in case bad weather or fog prevented him from attending. At the time of the constable's visit on March 11th the dog was under six months and as soon as it became necessary to take out a licence he applied for an exemption as a farmer of 250 acres on Skomer Island where the dog was normally kept.

Fined 5s.

Western Telegraph, Thursday, May 28th, 1936
SKOKHAM, NOT SKOMER ISLAND.
To the editor of the Telegraph.

Sir,—I see in your newspaper of May 21st an account of a case in which Mr Ronald Lockley was summoned with respect to a dog.

In your account you say that Mr Lockley wrote a letter from Skomer Island, and also that he applied for an exemption as a farmer of 250 acres on Skomer Island.

This is not so. Mr Lockley does not live on Skomer Island, but on Skokholm Island. To those who read the account it might seem to be otherwise. I should be glad if you would very kindly correct this mistake in your next issue.

Yours etc,

(Mrs) Betty Leyster Codd

Martin's Haven, Marloes, H-West.

Western Telegraph, June 4, 1936
The Pembrokeshire Islands
RIGHT OF ACCESS TO GRASSHOLM
To the Editor of the Telegraph

Sir,—Your reporter, after all, was only repeating history in confounding the names of the two islands, Skokholm and Skomer. But your correspondent, Mrs. Betty Codd of Marloes, who points out the mistake in your last issue, is herself in error in calling the island where I live Skokham. Perhaps, however, she is confusing the island with the lighthouse upon it. The lighthouse is officially Skokham lighthouse, but the island, according to the Ordnance Survey map, is Skokholm Island! A curious anomaly, but due, as I have been courteously informed by the Secretary to the Trinity Brethren, to the fact that the first enquiries for a lighthouse to be erected upon Skokholm came from the Bristol Chamber of Commerce, who in their correspondence called it in error Skokholm Island.

Both Skokham and Skomer are corrupted and therefore meaningless names, as I find by research through ancient deeds in the British Museum and the Public Records Office. All through the centuries from 1219 A. D. the records refer to the island of Skokholm in a variety of spellings, chiefly phonetic adaptations of the word Skokholm. In his charming book on 'Old Norse Relations with Wales' Mr B. G. Charles tells us that Skokholm is a Viking name coming from Skokkr—trees or logs in this case I surmise it means driftwood logs, since trees will not grow on the

island), and Holm—an islet, that is to say, the Islet of Driftwood
Logs. Perhaps the Vikings under Ubba in 878 A.D. gave this name
to the island because they found it well supplied with driftwood.
The true name of Skomer is Scalmey, from Scalme—a sword, and
ey - an island, literally the sabred or cloven island, because at one
point it is almost divided into two.

The island of Ramsey seems to be a corruption of Hrafn's Ey,
the Island of the Raven. While Grassholm is scarcely corrupted
from Grass-Holm, the grassy islet.

As far back as the aged men of today can remember Pembrokeshire fishermen and their forefathers before them had free access
to the lonely island of Grassholm, and landed and climbed about
the windswept uninhabited twenty acres of bird-strewn cliff and
grass which hide its volcanic rocks. According to tradition a trade
existed in the plucking and sale of the feathers of the puffins
which once—but do not now-nested in thousands there. However
that may be, it is true that fishermen lived at Grassholm in the fine
summer weather, mooring their boats in the little rocky gut in the
south-east cliff, and sleeping out in the long grass above this
natural harbour. There is more than one true tale of boats lost at
the moorings there in sudden storms, and of men marooned for
days as a result. So by usage the men of the sea established their
right of access to this outpost of Pembrokeshire.

Fishermen still go out to Grassholm, but perhaps because the
weather is (so the greybeards say) never so settled as of old, and
the fishing not so good (is anything ever so good as it was in the
'good old days' of youth?), they find fewer occasions to risk their
gear there. But a newer excuse to visit the islet has sprung up with
the increasing flow of summer visitors to Pembrokeshire, and the
fishermen's boats from St. Davids, Solva, Dale, Angle, even
Tenby, are chartered by these visitors to carry them out to
Grassholm for the purpose of seeing the fine colony of gannets
which year by year increases there. This, in view of the plight of
the lobstermen in the over-fished waters of Pembrokeshire, is all
to the good; a pound or two from this source will help to pay for
lost pots, new ropes, and engine, 'overheads.'

I feel sure, therefore, that all fishermen will join me in a note of protest against the attempt which is now being made to establish a monopoly in landing visitors at Grassholm by a certain boat at Marloes which advertises its claim to have that monopoly.

We know that the sea is, fortunately, free to all, and although it is true that the gannets and the seals of Grassholm can best be viewed from a boat below their rookeries, the sea journey there is a long one and many visitors are glad to get ashore for a rest there, as well as to get a closer view of the gannets. And I think that until it is legally proved otherwise, the fishermen, and through them the general public, have established their right by long usage to land on this desolate uninhabited rock in the sea. But to clear the matter up let us have all opinions. Perhaps through the courtesy of your columns this question might be discussed, and both laymen and legal opinion expressed. Then we who use small boats on the sea can be satisfied one way or the other, and bow to the final expression of the law. After all, the occasions when the weather and sea are calm enough to permit a landing at Grassholm are so few that it is imperative that the opportunity of viewing the birds and seals should not be restricted or denied those who have made long journeys from other parts of the British Isles in the hope of landing at Grassholm in boats from St. Davids, Solva, Angle, etc. Both the seals and the gannets are now so numerous and comparatively tame that there can be no likelihood of harm coming to them from such visits.

Personally, as an islander myself, I have always been ready to acknowledge the moral right of the owner of Grassholm by obtaining his approval, readily given, to land and to study and photograph sea-birds there. But this was nothing more than an exchange of courtesies, for in fact when my wife and I sailed there there was never a soul to challenge our landing, had anyone even the right to do so. Hence it came as a shock to us last year to be invited to pay Mrs Betty Codd 10s. for every time we, in our own boat, landed on Grassholm! But this year there are even more restrictions! Not only must you not land at Grassholm in your own boat, but you must go there in the aforesaid certain outboard motor boat from Marloes, and pay a minimum of £3 for the privilege!

I think it was W. H. Hudson who said (in effect) that he would never allow the accident of birth and possessions of any person to interfere with his full appreciation of the scene of nature wherever he chose to walk. But in this case the fishermen of Pembrokeshire have, as I maintain, the right of long usage behind them, and I am sure they will not allow it to be taken out of their hands withouth a fight for it.—'

Believe me, Yours &c.,
    Ronald M. Lockley.
Skokholm Bird Observatory.

Western Telegraph, June 11th, 1936
Right of Access to Grassholm.
To the Editor of the Telegraph.

Sir,—I should be obliged if you would grant me space in order to reply to a letter from Mr R. M. Lockley in last week's issue. I do not see what his statement that fishermen used formerly to go to Grassholm with their lobster pots has to do with the point at issue. In any case, no fishing has been carried on there for many years or, in fact, since the gannet colony became established there. The crux of the matter is that, though uninhabited, Grassholm is private property and, as the owner, I like to have some control over persons landing there. Does Mr Lockley suggest that private ownership means nothing and that any person, if so disposed, can contrary to the wishes of the owner enter on his property? Such a state of affairs would lead to anarchy. About the alleged right through usage, I should think it very doubtful.

Doubtless the fishermen of Pembrokeshire will feel greatly indebted to Mr Lockley for his disinterested efforts on their behalf but, as their rights have in no way been infringed, I fail to see why he should set himself up as their champion. Doubtless they are well able to look after their own interests. Mr Lockley has evaded the real issue, which is the objection I have to him, personally, taking his paying guests to Grassholm—my property—for fee or reward. Why should I allow him to land his guests on Grassholm without reference to me or, in my absence, to my daughter, Mrs Betty Codd of Martin's Haven? Despite his statement in his letter to your paper I have not stopped fishermen from taking parties to Grassholm.

It would be absurd to expect all visitors to North Pembrokeshire to go to Martin's Haven in order to engage a boat for the trip. At various times Messrs. Arnold, Mortimer and Beer of St Davids, have asked and obtained permission to take visitors both to Grassholm and Skomer. The only stipulation made is that they shall impress upon such visitors that the birds shall not be disturbed unduly.

Mr Lockley's real objection, then, seems to be founded not so much on altruistic concern for the fishermen as on a fear that he may lose what is perhaps a profitable service to himself, as he lives in the same neighbourhood. He was requested to allow such of his guests as wished to visit Grassholm to go in my daughter's boat. I do not feel that any apology is needed for wishing my daughter and her husband to profit from any traffic to Grassholm. If visitors to Pembrokeshire make long journeys from other parts of the British Isles in order to see the gannet colony, then surely it is not too much to expect them to behave with ordinary courtesy and to ask the owner's permission. Mr Lockley's recollection is at fault when he states that 10s had to be paid to Mrs Betty Codd every time he, in his own boat, went to Grassholm. The 10s. fee was only payable whenever he took a party of paying visitors to Grassholm. It was agreed that his personal friends should be exempt from such fee. Mr Lockley expects people who wish to go to Skokholm to consult him before they make the journey. Why, therefore, should he expect me to adopt different methods? And he is not even the owner of Skokholm, but the tenant. The Royal Society for the protection of Birds is on my side in this matter and Mrs Lenson, who has been connected with that Society for nearly 40 years, has written to Mr Lockley informing him of their opinion. They have some right to make this request as they are responsible for the rent of Skokholm Island.

Mr Lockley makes a large part of his living by journalistic work. It is, therefore, surprising that he should object to my daughter having the work of taking paying visitors to Grassholm, as he knows that such sums as may be earned by her and her husband form a considerable part of their income. In conclusion, far from desiring to hinder in any way the fishermen in their desire to add to their income, I have always put such work as I could in their way. The only Marloes fisherman who has to my knowledge visited Grassholm of recent years has been Mr Wm. Morris, and he had my consent to land some visitors there.

If there were more intending visitors than my daughter could take she would, of course, arrange with Mr Morris or such other fisherman as might be willing to work with her and her husband. —Yours, & c.,   W. F. Sturt.
Skomer Island, Marloes, Haverfordwest.

Western Telegraph, June 18th, 1936
Right of Access To Grassholm

To the Editor of the 'Telegraph.'

Sir—would you kindly allow me to reply to Mr Sturt's letter in your last issue? The facts submitted by him are not in accord with the challenge given me in person by his son-in-law, Mr Reuben Codd, who claimed, in a most aggressive fashion, the monopoly of landing visitors on Grassholm. It was because of this claim, covering, as he said, the whole of Pembrokeshire, that I thought it urgent to make the matter public, more especially as several fishermen had agreed with me that their rights were in danger. But if Mr Sturt says that he has no objection to fishermen landing people there, then all is well.

May I, however, clear up the other points mentioned by Mr Sturt? (1) Fishermen still fish at Grassholm, admittedly less regularly than of old, but certainly at some time every year, including this year, since men alive today can remember; (2) I do not take paying guests to Grassholm. Those who go are taken by fishermen in a large and powerful inboard motor-boat. I have, out of neighbourliness but not in recognition of any legal right,

offered them the opportunity of benefitting Mr Sturt's daughter by going in Mr Sturt's boat, manned by his son-in-law, but there seems to be a not unjustifiable objection to going too far out to sea in a small boat powered only by an outboard engine; (3) It has always been my pleasure to act as an unpaid Honorary Watcher for the Royal Society for the Protection of Birds, and if in return the Society has wished to make me some reward for those services (including the occasion when my wife and I were able to save the entire gannet coloy of Grassholm from a hideous death by fire in 1930, by sailing up to the flagship 'Renown' and claiming, successfully, the services of the British navy to land men and dig the fire out) by contributing a sum equal to my rent, nevertheless, the Society has no control over Skokholm, as Mr Sturt suggests, and I pay my own rent.—Yours etc,
    R. M. Lockley.
Skokholm Bird Observatory,
Dale, Haverfordwest.

Western Telegraph June 25th, 1936
Right of Access to Grassholm

Sir,—Would you very kindly allow me space for a final reply to Mr Lockley's letter with regard to free access to Grassholm, in your last issue.

I must confess I read with some amusement this last epistle of the 'champion' of the Pembrokeshire fishermen. I should view his efforts rather with surprise were his reasons not so easily understandable.

As Mr Lockley has been requested by the owner, Mr W. F. Sturt, to cease the visits to Grassholm of himself and his paying guests, he apparently thinks that by not making the journey in his own small boat (which he has always done up to now) but by hiring a certain fisherman's boat from Dale he can avoid the point by travelling in that boat and therefore, according to him, having the right of free access to Grassholm. Now perhaps we begin to establish certain rights for fishermen taking persons to Grassholm. Presumably the persons he has in mind are himself and his paying guests.

This attitude of friendly protection towards the 'helpless' fishermen is rather a new one on his part as I hear that up to now Mr Lockley has viewed with a most unfriendly eye all attempts by fishermen to land visitors at Skokham without his permission. I should say that what is sauce for the goose is sauce for the gander, and if Mr Lockely expects to land himself or anyone else on another man's island then I think anyone who wishes to should have the right of free access to Skokham.

It seems rather strange on Mr Lockely's part to have a notice board where visitors cannot fail to see it when they arrive at Skokham forbidding any person to land on the island without his permission. Mr Lockley seeks to prove that he or anyone else may land on Grassholm, yet is the first to prohibit anyone landing on the island he rents. Rather a curious attitude, to say the least.

Just one or two more points. Mr Lockley makes references to our 'small boat powered only by an outboard engine.' May I point out to him, as his memory seems strangely at fault, that our boat is capable of seating eight passengers in comfort, also three in crew; that we carry two engines in case of trouble to one; and that my husband and myself take an expert boatman on all our journeys to the island.

As the weather is always calm and peaceful when trips are made to Grassholm I fail to see where the danger lies. Of course we have not had Mr Lockley's narrow escapes from shipwreck, so perhaps we are not so capable of determining the hidden danger!

As for the 'large and powerful motorboat' in which Mr Lockley states his visitors are taken to Grassholm, can he be referring to the fisherman's boat from Dale that took certain of his paying guests and himself to Grassholm a week or so ago? If so, I should hardly refer to it as a reliable means of transport as I hear that this very excellent boat of which he speaks broke down just after the start of the return journey, drifted helpless for many long hours in the grip of wind and tide, and was at last given a tow by a friendly trawler to port. I should not like to guess at what hour the weary travellers returned home.

It seems rather extraordinary that Mr. Lockley should not care for the idea of visiting Grassholm 'in a small boat powered only by an outboard engine,' to quote from his letter, as ever since he first visited Grassholm, up to this summer, the only boat he has ever used for taking his paying guests and himself to Grassholm is his own boat, smaller than ours and powered only by a small outboard engine. In this small boat he and any man who happened to be working for him at the time have taken all his visitors to the island since first he went. May I ask why this sudden change of ideas with regard to size of boat required to visit Grassholm? Surely, if it was safe for Mr Lockley to visit the island in his boat with only one engine (whereas we carry a spare engine), it is quite in order for us to go there in our lifeboat which could not by any means be described as 'small.'

Of course I quite understand his desire to continue to take his visitors to Grassholm, as we all know that the bird population on Skokham is so small and seems to decrease in number every year that most of his visitors no doubt are attracted there only by the promise of a visit to Grassholm.

To finish—I fear Mr Lockley has not read my father's letter as he should. If I remember rightly, my father wrote in his letter that he had no objection to certain fishermen, whose names were stated, taking visitors to Grassholm as they had asked and received permisssion from him to do so. Not any fisherman as Mr Lockley seems to think. As for the fishermen who he stated agreed with him that their rights were in danger, to what rights did they refer? The rights of ownership? If so I think you will agree that the rights in this case certainly belong to the man who bought the island—namely, my father.

Yours, &c.,

Betty Leyster Codd.
Martin's Haven, Marloes,
Haverfordwest.
June 23rd, 1936.'

End of correspondence.

Now that, more recently, Grassholm has been immortalised with the designation of SSSI, ESA or something equally felicitous, it will be interesting to see whether attitudes remain the same. Especially since the seals and gannets are now even more numerous than they were fifty years ago when it was considered that they were 'So tame' that there could be 'no likelihood of harm coming to them from such visits.'

The other point of interest is the meaning of the name Skokholm. The suggestion of driftwood on Skokholm, especially at the time of the Vikings, was, of course, quite erroneous. The recognised authority, Dr. B. G. Charles, as I quoted in *The Sounds Between*, is on record as saying, 'The problem is to decide whether the Sc or St spellings are original. It is possible that the original form of Stokholm became Skokholm by assimilation and by analogy with the name of the neighbouring island of Skomer with which it was always coupled. Further, some of the Sc or St forms may be due to the common confusion of t and c in the transcription of mediaeval transcripts. Old Scandinavian stokkr meant 'a stock, trunk, log,' 'narrow bed of a river between two rocks'. In Scandinavian place-names the element was used of a sound, especially of a straight sound. Between Skokholm and Skomer there is a Broad Sound which may have been used by Scandinavian sailors on their trading voyages in these parts. The meaning 'island in the sound' is, therefore, probable.'

Chapter 4

The Seals

It has nothing to do with the Pembrokeshire islands but, up to the time of writing, we are living in a free country, or so they say, and I would like to quote a passage from that fascinating book, *The Islandman*, by Thomas O Crohan, published by Oxford University Press (1951) and translated by Robin Flower. It was written about O Crohan's life on the Blaskets, which would have been about the time when Vaughan Davies was on Skomer.

I have heard tales from the older people of how the seals, at one time, were taken for their flesh to eat although, within living memory, they were only taken for other purposes. The episode here recounted could well have been happening on the Pembrokeshire islands not all that long ago. When Browne Willis wrote of the seal-hunts on Ramsey in 1715 it is more than likely that the seals were being taken for human consumption.

'I had planned to have a rest when I had the turf cut and the shelter ready for throwing it in when it was dry; but I didn't get it, my lad! My father had always been a first-rate man in his youth and afterwards, and it was a constant saying of his that nobody ever got anything properly done who lay abed on the flat of his back when the sun was shining in the sky, and that it was bad for the health, too.

Well, whatever he was in the habit of saying, I had arranged with myself to have an extra bit of bed this morning before starting on another job. But before long I heard somebody talking aloud. A man spoke by the hearth and asked was Tom awake yet. My mother said no.

'Why do you ask?' says she.

'There's a boat going after seals,' says he.

The speaker was an uncle of mine on my mother's side. At first I thought it was my father speaking, but no—he had gone back to the strand.

I leapt up and, when I'd had a bite, crammed some food into my pocket and set out for the boat. All the rest were ready before me, with everything necessary to get the best of the seals: ropes to drag them out of the cave when they should be dead, and a big, stout club with a thick end to it—we should want that tight enough to lay them low. Off we went out of the creek.

Another boat had left early in the morning, but they had taken the direction of the Lesser Blaskets. They had fetched up at Inishvickillaun—a famous place for seals in the caves—for there are a lot of caves in that island.

You need calm weather and a good spring tide. Well, we put out the four oars, 'tough, sweet-sounding, enduring, white, broad bladed', as was the way with the boats of the Fenians of old so often, and stayed not from our headlong course till we reached the mouth of the cave we had fixed on.

The cave was in the western end of the Great Island. It was a very dangerous place, for there was always a strong swell round it, and it's a long swim into it, and you have to swim sidelong, for the cleft in the rock has only just room for a seal. When the boat stopped in the mouth of the cave there was a strong suck of swell running. Often and again the mouth of the hole would fill up completely, so that you'd despair of ever seeing again anybody who happened to be inside, and that left those of us who were in the boat little to say. The only young men there were myself and another lad, for the likes of us were not experienced enough for the job. It needs grown men, well on in years.

The captain of the boat spoke and said: 'Well, what did we come her for? Isn't anybody ready to have a go at the hole?'

It was my uncle who gave him his answer: 'I'll go in,' said he, 'if another man will come with me.'

Another man in the boat answered him: 'I'll go in with you', says he.

He was a man who stood in need of a bit of seal meat, for he spent most of his life on short commons. He had a big family, and none of them old enough to give him any help.

The two made their preparations. There was a bridge of rock across the mouth of the cave, with the water above and beneath

it. Two men had to stand on the bridge to help the other two in.
One of the two was a good swimmer, but not my uncle. The
swimmer went in first, carrying the end of the rope in his mouth,
the slaughtering stick under his oxter, a candle and matches in his
cap and the cap on his head. It was useless to go into the cave
without a light, for it penetrated too far under the ground. My
uncle followed him, another rope tied around him, and his hand
gripping the swimmer's rope, one end of which was tied up somewhere inside, while its other was fastened to the bridge outside so
as to be always ready.

The other youngster and I stayed on the bridge to drag out the
seals from the two inside. They kindled a light, and when they
reached the end of the cave, there was a beach full of seals there—
big and little, male and female. *Bainirseach* is the name of the
female seal, and the male is called the bull. There are some of
them that it's absolutely impossible to kill.

Seal Pup.

The two inside made themselves ready for the great enterprise before them. Each of them had a club, and they aimed a blow at every one of the seals. They had a lighted candle on a boulder. Both of them had a flannel shirt on, dripping, of course, from the salt water it had come through. When they had finished the slaughter and all the seals there were killed, they had more trouble in front of them. Many of the seals were very heavy, and the cave was a most awkward place: there were great boulders between them and the water, and the passage out was a very long one. But there's no limit to the strength a man has when he's in a tight place, and those two, handling the dead bodies of the seals there on the beach underground, worked like horses. They dragged every one of eight seals down to the water, and by the time they had done, the swell burst into the cave, and the two of us who were on the bridge had to grip the rock wall high up.

When that stress was past, there came a calm, and one of the men inside shouted to us to drag the rope out. We thought that one of themselves was on the rope, but it wasn't so. Four huge seals were tied to it. We had to pass the end of the rope to the boat, and, when the seals had been lifted in, to send it into the cave again. This rope was fastened to the rope that remained stretched into the cave, and the man who was with me on the bridge shouted out loud to them to draw it in again, and they did so in double quick time. Before long those inside called to us to drag it back again. The swell was raging mad by this. When we drew in the rope, there were four other seals tied to it, though we expected that it would be one of the men themselves. We had to do as we had done before and send the rope in again. Every now and then we were forced to leave the bridge from the great seas that swept over it, filling up the mouth of the cave too.

It was the swimmer who took to the rope first to make his way out, leaving it to the other man to use the fixed rope. It took the swimmer in the passage a long time to reach the bridge, there was so heavy a swell. He got there in the end, with his flannel shirt torn to tatters. My uncle—who, as I said before, couldn't swim a stroke—started on the last rope. The rise and fall and suck of the swell made it hard for us to pull him to the bridge. In the middle of it all, the rope broke, and the wave swept him back with it into the cave again. My heart was in my mouth when I saw him going down. I thought he was lost. I plunged down from the bridge into the submerged cave. My foot struck the end of the broken rope under the water. By God's grace I brought off my good uncle safe and sound, but we had a desperate struggle for it. I was a good swimmer in those days.

Our big boat was loaded down to the gunwale with four cow seals, two bulls, and two two-year-olds—one for each of the crew. Every one of the men had a barrelful of seal meat, and we reckoned in those days that every barrel of seal meat was worth a barrel of pork. The skins fetched eight pounds.

It's odd the way the world changes. Nobody would put a bit of seal meat in his mouth to-day. They melt it down for light, for it is cram-full of oil. Moreover, if you made a present of the skin to a gentleman, he'd hardly deign to accept it from you. It's long since anybody tried to do anything with one of them but throw it to the dogs. Yet in those days they were a great resource for the people, both the skin and the meat, and you could get a pack of meal for one of them. And anywhere you liked to take a lump of seal's flesh you could get the same weight of pork for it, if there were any in the house. People don't know what is best for them to eat, for the men that ate that kind of food were twice as good as the men of to-day. The poor people of the countryside were accustomed to say that they fancied they would live as long as the eagle if they but had the food of the Dingle people. But the fact is that the eaters of good meat are in the grave this long time, while those who lived on starvation diet are still alive and kicking.'

Those were indeed hard times on the Blaskets, where some of the Irish peasants had gone during the dark days in Ireland's history, at the time of the potato famines, to try to get away from the rapaciousness of the landlords, and to scratch some sort of meagre living. It would be hard people indeed who would criticise or condemn them for the slaughter they perpetrated.

In previous books I have told how the fishermen round the Pembrokeshire islands used to destroy the seals at every possible opportunity in the old days, and there are folks who raise their hands in horror at such a thought. But the fishermen have a point-of-view. The salmon fishermen also, I believe, are increasingly concerned at the depredations of the seals as they wait for the salmon at the river estuaries preparing for their seasonal runs up river to spawn. In addition to that there is the incidence of worm infestation as a result of worms carried and transmitted by the seals.

In 1979 L. Harrison Matthews published a book, entitled *The Seals and the Scientists*, (Peter Owen Ltd) in which he writes of work he did on seal research round the Pembrokeshire islands. The first of Dr Matthews' sorties occurred when he stayed on Skomer at the time of the Invasion of 1946. He tells how Ronald Lockley took them round the bays of the island trying to shoot a seal but without success, so then they went to Ramsey. Even there they met with no success until,

'We gathered up our dunnage and scrambled back up the ravine to the summit where we paused to get our breath and take a last look at the distant Bishop on his lonely rock, and the surf breaking on the pebbles in the empty cove below, before turning to tramp back over the island to the landing place where the ship lay. On our way over the eastern slopes we stopped for a moment at the house to say goodbye to the tenant, and then went on down the winding track towards the harbour. Syd was a little ahead of us when he reached the last bend on the cliff edge between the Waterings and the harbour; he stood looking down into the waters of Ramsey Sound as he waited for us to catch up with him.

Suddenly he started and stood rigid for a moment; he dropped his haversack, crouched down and hurried back towards us.

'Here, give us that rifle quick!' he whispered hoarsly, 'there's one down there in the water.'

He hastily grabbed and loaded the rifle, and ran quietly to the cliff edge. We crept up to him as he stood with the rifle to his shoulder taking aim at something below. A seal's head showed above the surface about a hundred yards out; it was a very small target bobbing in the waves at that distance, and it quietly disappeared beneath them as Syd was trying to sight on it.

'You'll never hit it as far as that,' said Ronald. 'And if you did it would sink.'

'Bide still,' Syd replied. 'She'll be up again in a minute.'

As he spoke the seal reappeared, not just sticking its nose out, but swimming slowly on the surface with the curve of its back awash. As it raised its snout Syd fired, and its head fell forward with a splash.

'Got him, by God!' shouted Alister, springing up and dashing down the path to the harbour, closely followed by the rest of us.

Syd took a flying leap into the boat and started cranking the engine while Alister and I cast off fore and aft and tumbled in after him as he put her in gear with a slam that nearly pulled her stern under. He put the tiller hard over and we swept away from the quay leaving Ronald and Alan yelling at us to hurry.

'Stand by with that gaff!' Syd shouted. 'It's with the boat-hook on the cabin top.'

We pulled it out from its lashing and ran forward. The seal was floating just under the surface in the middle of a huge crimson

Seals basking.

patch which was spreading wider and wider as the corpse began to sink slowly beneath it. Syd throttled back and brought us gently alongside, Alister standing on the gunwale and leaning overside, hanging onto the shrouds with his left hand and holding the gaff ready in his right. I grabbed him by the arm as he swung with all his weight outboard and neatly hooked the seal under the flipper.

'Okay!' I called to Syd, heaving Alister back.

Syd gave her a touch astern to take the way off, put the engine out of gear and ran forward to help.

'Don't try to lift her out or the gaff'll draw,' he said. 'Work her alongside to the cockpit and we'll get a line on.'

He slipped a running bowline over the hind flippers and drew it tight above them, and we all tailed onto the rope. It was easy enough to heave the body half out but then it got very heavy; Alister and I got hold of a front flipper on each side while Syd kept the strain on the rope, his feet braced on the cockpit coaming; with a struggle the three of us worked it up over the gunwale onto the side deck.

'Avast heavin',' said Syd, threading a length of cod line through the waterways to lash it down.

Alister made a quick examination of its hind end.

'It's a female all right,' he said. 'Just what we wanted. That was a marvellous shot of yours.'

'Aye,' replied Syd, 'I wouldn't promise to do that every time. We were damn lucky to save it, they nearly always sinks.'

He started the engine and turned back to the harbour.

'She would have done if she'd been standing upright in the water like they often do,' I said. 'It was only because her body was flat on the surface and her head fell down that the air didn't all rush out of the lungs, and so she kept afloat. If you hit them when they're upright all the wind blows out and they sink like a stone.'

'It's a female!' Alister called to the others as we came alongside the quay. 'Couldn't be better.'

'What about catching that train?' Ronald asked. 'You'll hardly make it now.'

'We won't,' I replied, 'but that don't matter.'

'It'll take some time to dissect it and pickle the bits we want,' Alister said. 'And they must be taken out while they're fresh, they'll be no good if they're stale.'

'What we'd better do,' said Ronald, 'is to take it over to Porth Stinian and give you a hand with it to the top. You can do your stuff there and then phone to St David's for a car to take you to Haverfordwest. We'll have to leave you or we won't get back to Skomer till after dark. That okay?'

It suited us, so we embarked all the gear and ran across the Sound to the lifeboat slip at Porth Stinian where we unloaded everything and got it all to the top of the cliff on the little trolley hauled up on a wire cable.

'Well, there you are,' Ronald said, when it was all safely up. 'Good luck with it. We must get moving or we'll not get back tonight.'

Ronald and Syd went down to the ship while we sorted out the things we should need for our dissection and made a dump of the rest. By the time we had pulled the seal to a level bit of turf and were ready to begin, the *Shearwater* was disappearing round the headland at the south end of Ramsey Sound and setting course for Skomer.'

Subsequently Dr Matthews and some colleagues returned and managed to catch a seal cow and her new-born pup, and weighed the pup for a number of weeks, before allowing them to return to sea. Later Dr Matthews tells how Professor Hewer shot a number of seals on Ramsey before achieving his objective of shooting a gravid seal. There are still those who talk of the cutting up, disembowelling and butchering in general that went on at that time.

Useful information may have been collected as a result of it, but I can almost hear the voice of the late Reuben Codd as he would undoubtedly have asked, 'But would the seals be any better off because of it?'

I fancy it will be a long time before such happenings again occur on the Pembrokeshire islands, and there are some who will not be sorry.

Chapter 5

Ramsey

I met R. G. (Phil) Davies, who was then on Ramsey, at the time when Brinley Hooper was building the new bungalow on Skomer. Phil had acquired an army D.K.W. 'Duck', and he came down from Ramsey to ferry the building materials across to Skomer from Martinshaven. A few years later Brinley was also to re-build the farm-house on Ramsey when the late K.P. Allpress bought the island. Phil suggested to me that Ramsey would also be a good place to stay and, the year after I had paid that brief visit to Skokholm, I took him at his word, as a result of which I was there at the time when he was at variance with his new landlord, and I became involved in the negotiations, at the satisfactory conclusion of which the Davies family left the island.

The "Duck" landing building materials for the new house on Skomer.

Brinley Hooper's men re-building the farmhouse on Ramsey.

Before that, however, in the autumn of 1962, I spent a week-end there, wrote one of my weekly columns on the affair, and give you my solemn assurance that every word of it is true, apart from the fact that I did actually volunteer to go in the boat when otherwise Phil's teenage daughter would have had to have gone with him.

We had gone to Ramsey on the Friday evening. On the Saturday morning Phil had crossed to St Justinian's to collect two more visitors, ond on returning to the island, had left the boat in the little harbour by the jetty, instead of taking her out to her moorings at the Waterings. The tide was on the ebb and, by the time there was again enough water in the harbour for the boat to float, there was a force twelve gale blowing and the boat was being battered on the rocks. I can only say, in retrospect, that there are more comfortable places to be than in a motor-boat in Ramsey Sound in a force twelve gale.

'October 6th, 1962.

If this ever sees the light of day you will know that all is well, more or less, even if it is only just, because at one time it looks as if I will never be writing a column for you ever again.

You will remember that the last time I write a little piece for you I am generally just a little bit fed up with one and all and therefore I decide to take a few days to get in some heavy work on the old peace and quiet lark because I am a great believer in this at all times as being a very good cure for many ailments including being run down, tired, overworked and other such distressing maladies.

That is why I explain to you I am going away to this island where I can watch the seals and that, and I leave in such great haste that I have no time to write a little piece for you before I go. What is more I cannot even think what there is for me to write about. The well is dry. I am, as the saying goes, bereft of reason and am without inspiration in any shape or form.

However, I do not let this worry me unduly because I am a great believer in a spot of peace and quiet to rectify such matters, and I decide I will maybe write a little piece for you whilst I am on this island in my own good time and do not rush these matters.

Anyway everything goes all right and we reach this island in considerable safety but with not much to spare as it is somewhat rough at the time. I would also ask you to take note of this use of the first person pronoun in the plural as you might say because I am not alone.

In fact we are very much in the plural. There is one character who has a slipped disc and is in very poor shape generally and I cannot see even a very large amount of peace and quiet putting him right. He also has a little bottle from which he has to put drops into his eyes every few hours and in addition to this he has many cameras and accompanying impedimenta in order to take photographs of the seals and the peace and quiet and all this and that.

There is also one small badger very much present and correct because he wishes to learn about these matters and in any case he thinks that life on an island must be fun. That's a laugh that is. I'll tell you. That's a laugh.

Needless to say Mrs Brock will not be very happy to allow this small badger to travel alone with a parent in search of peace and quiet and such characters as go about the place with cameras and slipped discs putting drops in their eyes. It is therefore very easy to persuade Mrs Brock that she will very much enjoy such a quiet week-end as that of which I am now about to speak.

Well, everything goes along very nicely and there is much peace and quiet everywhere and a lot of fresh air very sweet and whole-some all about the place and the sun is shining in spite of the fact that it is blowing very hard. So the first morning we are here I go with this other character and the small badger to take some of these pictures of all these seals and their pups.

We use this rope to get down the steep track down this cliff and end up on a pebbly beach with the wild waves pounding and seals everywhere to be seen. Then we go into a big dark cave and, of course, I am carrying the camera for this other character as he is in great trouble on these pebbles on account of his slipped disc.

Once we are inside the cave I climb up on a big boulder which is very greasy on account of the sea and darkness and all that and immediately fall lens over shutter and plunge about ten thousand feet onto my back. It is very painful.

Even so this other character thinks it is all highly amusing and a great diversion from thinking about his slipped disc and he speeks as follows: 'It is a great shame' he says, 'That I do not have a camera ready.' He says, 'I think it will be great fun ha-ha to take a picture of you in such a position.' But it is some time before he can say all this because of his great amusement.

Anyway we manage to get back up the cliff and back to the farmhouse for dinner and, apart from the head boss man of this place and his family, there are also two other characters, male and female, who just arrive in search of peace and quiet and likewise also some pictures and it is in every way a very welcome and enjoyable meal and, like the boy scout's pastry, well cooked.

The only thing that spoils the meal for me is the great lack of manners of all the other characters round the table including my own nearest and dearest because they all take great delight in making mock of affliction and they are far more amused by the description of my fall as given by the fool with the slipped disc than they are sympathetic on account of my own great suffering.

I explain that I have in fact broken a finger in this fall, so they say how can I now write my column for the newspaper so that I then point out I have only broken the finger in my left hand which they agree is not at all important as it will not prevent me writing my column.

Even so it is necessary for me to go to bed for what is known as a nap and I think that by the time I wake up I will maybe have some inspiration to write a column for you. So I do this and in spite of the fact that there is a great gale blowing I go to sleep. Very soon, however, I am awakened by a great shouting from the beach below.

It is the head boss man of this island and he is in a great state of agitation so I grab some shoes and a large mackintosh because it is now raining very furious and I dash to help him. Unfortunately, on the the greasy bank my feet go from under me and I suffer another great fall in exactly the same place including my arm and elbow.

But there is no time to bother about this because the boat is being pounded on the rocks by great waves and it is most distressing. So the head boss man says I must go with him in the boat and as I am such a simple soul who should not be allowed out without his mamma and as I cannot think of any quick excuse like having a wife and family, until it is too late, I jump into the boat and fall on the same elbow and arm again.

We get the engine going and get her off the rocks and we manage to get out to the mooring where there are great chains and all this and that fastened to a buoy for keeping a boat at such times as this. But once we are there we find we cannot get back

against the wind in a rowing boat because the wind is blowing
about a thousand miles and hour.

The head boss man says to me 'You cannot swim can you?' So
I look at him very hurt and say 'Do you not hear that in my time
I am a very great swimmer with medals and certificates and all
that and, in fact, I cleave through the water like an arrow. But that
is many years ago,' I say, 'and I do not think I will do very much
cleaving like an arrow in my present state of health.'

'Never mind,' says the head boss man. 'It is like riding a bicycle.
Once you learn how to do it you will never forget it. Even so,' he
says, 'I think we will now put lifejackets on.'

So we do this and I cannot help thinking that if we do land up
in the drink the seals will be greatly perplexed at what we are
supposed to be doing, especially in these outfits.

In fact at this time they are dodging all round in the sea and
looking at us most surprised and they are no doubt thinking that
human beings are very odd creatures but, of course, they do not
understand about peace and quiet and such matters.

Then the head boss man says 'Do you think you now have
enough to write about in your column?' and I say, 'Yes, if you will
please take me back to the island or anywhere out of this mayhem
I will now be pleased to make an immediate start on the writing.'

I also say that if it was half as bad as this at the time they tried
to cross the dark and stormy waters then Lord Ulin's daughter
and the Chief of Ulva's Isle must have been a couple of nut cases.

By this time it is getting dark as well as raining and blowing, but
there is a great amount of white everywhere, which is the foam
and the spray of the waves which are pounding us every which
way. The rowing boat has also filled with water and gone to the
bottom and I do not at this time give much for my chances of ever
writing a column for you again.

As we see the oars of the dinghy wash away in the gloom I
understand the meaning of the expression 'up the creek without
a paddle.'

The head boss man says the boat weighs a couple of tons but he
does not take into account that she is bows under and has shipped
about ninety five tons of water. However it is now high tide so we

get the engine going again and make one last desperate run for it against the wind and tide.

The next thing I know I am up on the jetty with a rope in my hand and, of course, I have landed on the same elbow and arm again but there is no time to dwell on such matters as the head boss man is shouting his head off for me to pull on the rope like hallejlulah glory be and, of course, he is not taking the ninety five tons of water into account.

Immediately, the character with a slipped disc, followed by the other characters male and female loom up out of the darkness and we get the ropes onto the big winch and there is much turning and heaving as is both customary and necessary at such times not to mention a great deal of shouting and such like.

In the middle of it something goes wrong and the winch handle swings round and cops me a fourpenny on the same arm and elbow which makes me see about twenty seven thousand stars of different colours shapes and sizes.

It is evident by this time that I will finish up with nothing less than gangrene but I am so wet and cold I do not let it bother me. There is sea water running out through my earholes, and my eyes are red raw from the salt water.

It is well after midnight before we know that the boat is safe and then I drink four times as much rum as anyone else because it is recognised that I am on the delicate side and they all assure me it is a certain antidote against gangrene.

That is about all there is to the story except to state that the other character on the winch with me is the character with the slipped disc. When he manages eventually to striaghten up he finds that his slipped disc is greatly improved. In fact I think he will now be fit to carry his own cameras.

What is more he is open to receive offers for his bottle of eyedrops because all the salt water from the waves breaking over him has put him as good as new and his eyes are perfect again and obviously very healthy. The salt water is very healing.

Futhermore I have all the inspiration I need for a column thank you very much and this explains why I am such a great believer in all this peace and quiet as a certain cure for complaints various.'

How we winched the boat out of the water that night I shall never know. Perhaps it was a case, as Thomas O Crohan said, 'There's no limit to the strength a man has when he's in a tight place.'

We came off in a smaller boat on the Tuesday morning, and arrived home to find that our glass front door had been smashed during the gale. As we walked into the house the 'phone rang. It was my father, who said, 'Oh, you're home at last then.'

Apparently Reuben Codd had called to see us on the Sunday evening and was rather mystified to be greeted by an empty house with the front door blown in. He was standing amidst the debris in the hall wondering what it was best to do when the 'phone rang. He answered it and played canny. It was my father and he, hearing a strange voice answer, also kept the cards close to his chest. Eventually they established each other's identity and laughed over it. Reuben told Father about the door and he said, 'The dull bugger's gone to Ramsey for the week-end. All three of 'em have gone.'

'Ah well,' said Reuben who had some small knowledge of such matters as crossing to and from the islands, 'you won't see anything of them for a couple of days.' And they didn't.

When I was researching *The Sounds Between* the late Tommy Warren Davies asked me whether I had come across any reference to Welsh Black bees on Ramsey. In spite of the many questions I asked during the three years I was working on the book I came across not a word about them. Then, back in 1983, I was invited as guest speaker to the annual dinner of the Pembrokeshire Bee-keepers Association. Why they should have invited me I cannot for the life of me think. It was certainly nothing to do with what I could possibly know about bees.

However, I thought I could fly a kite, or start a hare, or whatever the term is, and mentioned Ramsey and the Welsh Black bees. Sure enough, at the bar afterwards, a gentleman came up to me and said the man to tell me all about it would be P.C. Wren. The retired policeman, who had acted as foul-brood officer to the

Ministry of Agriculture, was not, in fact, able to tell me all that much, but he put me on the right trail.

The old *Farm News* had ceased publication in 1969. In 1983 another paper, *Farming Wales*, was launched upon an unsuspecting and, as it transpired, an ungrateful nation and they asked me if I would resurrect my old Ben Brock column. It was a bit more fun for the short while it lasted and Ben Brock contributed an item on Ramsey and Welsh Black bees.

'January, 1984—

Do you, by any chance, know anything about bees?

If you don't, you're in good company, for neither do I, and I hope and trust you will take my word for it.

On the other hand, if you do happen to know anything about bees, there will be no need for you to take my word for it that I do not know anything about them, because it will very soon become evident, since I propose to write about them.

Not that there is any law against characters writing or speaking about things about which they know nothing, and that is why there is such great foolishness being written and spoken here and there and round and about generally.

In fact, it makes me think that, as we have so many laws, maybe there would be no harm in having one more law to prevent characters writing and speaking about things of which they know nothing and then we could have a bit of peace and quiet about the place generally and save some of the paper which is now being wasted.

However, like I said, there is no law against it, and so I am going to write about bees.

Of course, I do not want to write about bees as such, to use a phrase much loved by the sort of characters who go about the place saying hopefully.

Neither do I wish to write about bees in general, except to say that I know they mate whilst flying, so they must be contortionists or acrobats or something, and even that depends on the drone being able to fly high enough to catch up with the queen and then he drops dead from all the exertion and the birds eat him up.

So there isn't much percentage in being a bee, especially if you're a worker bee, because then you don't get any fun at all, and people come and steal the honey, which is just about the same as being nationalised.

So, what with one thing and another, you can say it's a hard life for a bee at that.

Wherefore and therefore, whilst I do not wish to write about bees as such, or bees in general, I wish to write a few words about Welsh Black bees in particular.

Never mind how I first became mildly interested in the subject but, about twenty years or more ago, I was doing some research concerning the Pembrokeshire islands.

And a very fine old gentleman with a great love for, and knowledge of, country things, asked me had I ever come across anything concenring Welsh Black bees on the islands.

He had an idea that he had once heard something about Welsh Black bees on Ramsey and that the last known colony of the native indigenous bees had been located on that lovely island.

I found nothing in any records and, as so often happens, was not lucky enough to ask the right questions of the right people at the right time.

And those who could have told me have long since been called Home and are collecting their honey in the heather-clad hills of sunnier climes.

But, some folks reckon, Heaven won't be such a marvellous place at that if they also happen to have any Welsh Black bees there. A fearsome species, by all account.

It seems there were definitely some in the Fishguard area of North Pembrokeshire over half a century ago because a chap brought his bees down with him from England, and the local bees killed the lot.

Memory plays funny tricks. I know that. And the people who do remember what happened on Ramsey have slightly differing versions.

One thing I know for sure, though. The bees were put there by the late Dr Evan Edwards, who was at that time an entomologist at University College at Cardiff.

With the advent of war, his wife thought it would be no bad plan to keep bees to help out with the sugar ration.

One of her husband's colleagues, the late Dr. T. I. Davies, urged her on and her husband, of course, also became interested.

Subsequently—and how it came about I don't know—Dr Edwards was asked by Miss Jane Humphries, a beekeeper, of Penrhyndeudraeth, in North Wales, whether he could help to save the Welsh Black bee from extinction by taking a hive of her stock.

They had been kept by her grandfather, and his grandfather before that, and way back for generations.

It seems that, as a result of the ravages of 'Isle of Wight disease' back about 1912, something like ninety percent of our own bees were wiped out and subsequently many new strains of bees were brought in from various countries.

There are still, they say, a few colonies of bees to be found which carry something of the characteristics of the Welsh Black bee but, as Tom Collings, that very knowledgeable beekeeper of Ciliau Aeron, says, 'How can you tell for sure? How can you prove it?'

Anyway Dr. Edwards had the rather bright idea of putting Miss Humphries' Welsh Black bees on Ramsey, and the farmer at that time, a most loveable man, the late Bertie Griffiths, was quite willing to cooperate.

It would be a good place to keep the stock pure, there was plenty of heather, and it would be interesting to see whether any of them would cross to the mainland.

Round about 1948, Dr Edwards was contemplating a future with the Ministry of Agriculture, which would have meant the NAAS.

He was not too happy, however, at what was happening and took up an appointment in Ghana instead. He came back about 1962 and died the following year.

So far I have heard three versions of what happened.

One is that when he came back and went to Ramsey to see about the bees, he was told that somebody had taken them away a year or two previously.

He was very upset about it and never found out what became of them.

I am not much inclined to accept this version because I am assured that he never went back to Ramsey following his return from Ghana.

The more likely story is that, not being any great bee-keeper, he gave it up as a bad job and destroyed the bees before he left for Ghana.

Who better to remember than Dr Edwards' widow, who assured me that was so?

On the other hand, Mr Griffiths' son Elfed, who was a boy on Ramsey at the time, assures me that the bees, considerably fewer in numbers by the end of it all, were definitely taken from the island and not destroyed there.

So what did become of the native Welsh Black bees, vicious customers that they were?

Are there any still about?

Or is it really true what it says in the Good Book that the meek shall inherit the earth?'

It has previously been remarked that, from such facts as are available, it is reasonable to suggest that the same sort of thing has been happening throughout the centuries on all three islands of Ramsey, Skomer and Skokholm at any one time. That is to say, one housheold on each, the type of farming, exploitation of the rabbits, decline of farming fortunes, and an increasing awareness of wildlife, with the eventual establishment of study and a degree, however misguided in certain cases, of protection. Even on distant, tiny Grassholm, now in the hands of the Royal Society for the Protection of Birds, sheep were once kept at a time when the keeping of sheep on all the islands was profitable.

It seems odd to wonder whether it only took the antics of one silly little man to change the course of history, and who can ever answer such a hypothetical question?

When I wrote in *The Sounds Between* of the acquisition of Ramsey by the late Peter Allpress in 1959, whose intention it was to let the island to a farmer with an interest in wild life and conservation, I said, 'Even on the mainland it is no easy task to make farming pay, and the man on the island has additional problems with which to contend. To what extent there can be a reconciliation between the interests of the wildlife protectionist and the farmer who has to produce to the utmost of his capacity is something which, as yet, remains to be seen.'

The short answer is that the idea did not succeed. After R. G. Davies had left in the autumn of 1963, he was followed for a short time by T. C. Dunn, who went there to farm the island and act as Honorary Warden. He, in turn, was followed, again for a short time, by Richard Alison, who tried to farm the island, whilst a warden for the Royal Society for the Protection of Birds was installed in the re-furbished bungalow at Ysgubor. The result was anything but a success.

When the warden had gone a young man by the name of Robin Pratt, who had been working for the Alisons, took over as warden and went to live in the bungalow. When the Alisons left, the R.S.P.B. were subsequently given a seven year lease. Ramsey was now a full-blown nature reserve with all the nonsense the name so often implies to those who know anything about it. Everything, so far, was in accord with the march of time.

What happened altogether I do not pretend to know, and I do not suppose for one moment that anybody ever will know. But one thing I do know, and that is that it was the full intention of Peter Allpress that Ramsey should be a nature reserve for all time. He was first of all a farmer and countryman who, through circumstances, became a successful and wealthy businessman. He retained his farming interests and love of the country, and had a great interest in bird protection. He was very active with the R.S.P.B. for whom, as chairman of their finance committee, he had done excellent work.

He died with tragic suddeness in the spring of 1968 when he was only fifty years of age. A short time before that I spent a few hours with him and his wife, Joy, at their bungalow at St Justinian's. We talked of Ramsey's more recent history and he told me that he was making arrangements for the future of the island. His actual words were, 'So if anything should happen to me next week, Ramsey is safe to the R.S.P.B. for ever.'

In the event he died, metaphorically speaking, not next week, but tomorrow. He was out in Libya with other R.S.P.B. people at the time. As so often has happened in such cases, his personal affairs had not all been put in order, and the arrangements for Ramsey had not been finalised.

Shortly afterwards his widow, still terribly distressed, was at St. Justinian's when one of the 'head sherangs' of the R.S.P.B. pulled in with his car, towing his caravan, which he then proceeded to park in front of the house. To say the least Mrs Allpress, her Celtic blood aroused, was not best pleased and asked him what he thought he was doing. The silly little man was anything but polite, and Mrs Allpress felt constrained to point out to him that the island did not belong to the R.S.P.B.—yet!

The trouble with so many of these birdy and conservationist types is that they seem to think they are God's gift to a grateful nation, and that wildlife and all within the countryside has been placed there for their special delectation, that they and only they know anything about it, and that none shall say them nay.

Do not misunderstand me. There are some splendid and dedicated people of great knowledge who work in this field and I have nothing but respect and admiration for them. But it is rather like the C.N.D., where some lovely well-meaning, Christian people find all the lefty loonies and anarchists in creation jumping on the band-wagon with them.

I remain convinced that it was with the incident of the caravan that the rot set in.

It was a time also of colossal expansion. The R.S.P.B. which had for long been a society of manageable, reasonable numbers, and doing much useful work, suddenly increased by thousands and became big business, with all the key-rings, ballpoint pens, teacloths and mementomania concomitant with such developments. At nature reserves hides were built, and car parks, where those who used the hides could park their cars. It is all part of the great leisure and environment growth industry with its maps and interpretive literature. Wardens were expected to alert the society to the names of members who were 'good for' donations and bequests.

Robin Pratt had left both the island and the R.S.P.B. and gone to work elsewhere which he did for a number of years.

On Ramsey the pattern developed true to type where the emphasis was on income from the numbers who could visit the island. And that was not the worst of it. With a complete lack of any sense of responsibility, gates and the doors of farm-buildings were broken up for firewood with the same total disregard as that with which the beautifully preserved bacon-oven had been vandalised on Skomer when the conservationists initially got their hands on it in 1959. All in all the trustees to the Allpress estate were far from happy at the way things were going. At the end of the seven years the R.S.P.B.'s lease was not renewed.

In the meantime Robin Pratt had married Judy, a daughter of Peter Allpress, and gone back to the R.S.P.B., first at Minsmere and then in Kent, before being sent back to Ramsey. It was then that they heard that the R.S.P.B. lease was not being renewed so they applied to the trustees themselves and were given a long lease. That was in 1975.

Robin and Judy Pratt on Ramsey before their Marriage.

So, Ramsey moved out of the general pattern which had seemed to have been its destiny, and farming was again to be the order of the day. The economics of trying to farm an off-shore island were dealt with extensively in *The Sounds Between*, along with the experiences of so many of those who had made the effort over the years. Not since the days of Bertie Griffiths had it been possible to make a living farming by traditional methods. And he had farmed on Ramsey in an age when it was still possible to call on help occasionally from neighbours and family on the mainland.

The new tenants recognized many of the difficulties inherent in the situation. Sheep, of course, were a natural and inevitable foundation for any farming policy, but it was a time when the return per acre from sheep was so poor that Ministry of Agriculture advisers were telling farmers to get rid of them.

They needed another enterprise and, thinking out all the options, decided to introduce a herd of red deer. History had repeated itself. They knew, from Fenton's account, that there had been red deer on Skokholm in the eighteenth century, but they did not know then that there had also been red deer on Skomer in the nineteenth. Possibly there have been deer on Ramsey, evidence of which is still waiting to be discovered. But one thing we know for sure is that none of the deer in those cases would, like those of the Pratts, have been flown there by helicopter.

Change, however, is written on all earthly things, and the Pratts quickly recognized that deer farming itself was becoming a rapidly expanding enterprise requiring chilled rooms and other such sophistications. It did not seem to make good sense on a leased farm to spend the money this would entail.

There was, too, the prospect ahead of two children to be schooled and a third one expected. It is a question which has entered into islanders' considerations since time out of mind, and the decision was taken to relinquish the unexpired part of their lease and to take their deer to a farm which they bought in the lovely Gwaun Valley of north Pembrokeshire. And at that stage the trustees put Ramsey up for sale.

Tranquillised Red Deer being landed on Ramsey by the Royal Navy's Helicopter.

I came to know John Freeman because of a serious affliction he has in common with the Abbot of Caldey. They both claim to suffer from a frozen right hand. They hate writing letters.

I was over on Caldey a few years ago, and talking to the Abbot in his office, when he pushed a letter across the desk to me and said, 'What d'you make of that?'

The letter was from John Freeman, and was really a cry from the heart asking the Abbot how they had managed to get rid of the rabbits on Caldey. He really would like to know, for Ramsey was swarming with them.

'You know all about this,' Fr Robert said. 'You write to him.'

And so, for the first time in twenty years, I went to Ramsey again. The last time I had been there was the day Richard Alison and his family moved in. The fields were as bare as a baby's bottom, as they say in Pembrokeshire, and the place was literally lifting with rabbits.

John Freeman and his wife, Alison, did not go to Ramsey in search of the good life, or to get away from it all. They went by chance and to do a job of work. Norfolk born, the Freemans must have looked slightly less likely candidates than many to succeed in such a venture. Having taken his M.A. degree in English at Cambridge, John Freeman took up a career in merchant banking. Then he met his future wife, who was working as a journalist, and, when she studied in Cardiff, he joined her there, they married, and opened an antiquarian bookshop.

It was something new to both of them, but they made a success of it, and then John was asked by an old friend of his University days, Henry Sebestyen, to join him in a farming venture in which he was interested. The farming deal, however, fell through and, at that point, they heard that Ramsey was for sale. They had gone as far as to make an offer for the island when Henry died suddenly and tragically. At that stage his family took over and set up a Trust, bought the island in his memory, and his ashes are buried there.

The Freemans went to Ramsey in 1981. Their first boy, Griff, was born that year and Thomas was born in 1984.

Knowing little enough about farming they quite wisely decided to follow the example of the Pratts and went in for deer and sheep. There was also the question of the rabbits with which the island had become infested. They robbed the sheep of what little grass there was, and ravaged the trees which were planted in an attempt to form windbreaks and shelter belts. A great deal of fencing has been done and 7,000 pine trees have been planted. One season's severe drought was no more helpful than the rabbits.

Initially there was also no small degree of confusion caused by the conservationists. When they moved in the newcomers suddenly found themselves being bombarded with letters from all the Societies, Trusts, Councils and Commissions in creation. Not knowing much about the subject they thought it seemed like a good idea to convene a meeting.

John Freeman and Alison with Griff and Thomas.

Red deer on Ramsey.

John Freeman said, 'The only one with any sense was David Saunders, and he didn't say anything much.' In that company he was a wise man.

When they asked for advice on how to get rid of the rabbits, in order to improve the farming and botancial variety of the island, a character from the Nature Conservancy Council replied, 'Why don't you farm the rabbits? They would keep the grass closely grazed for the choughs.'

So the Freemans pointed out that sheep would do that adequately, and added that they had already been told by another N.C.C. official that it was precisely because of rabbit infestation that the Pembrokeshire islands had been reduced to a botanical slum.

Next came the question of the trees for shelter belts for the stock and to help and to increase the bird-life. There are now trees growing on Skomer which Reuben planted down by the North pond in the 1950's. And there are some very lovely trees which enhance the beauty of Caldey. The only contribution a young lady ecologist could offer, however, was to say that she loved to drive down to St Justinian's of an evening and sit in her car and admire the profile of Ramsey against the sunset, and that further-more she was determined that trees should not spoil the outline of the island.

Somebody else said they could not possibly condone the commercial exploitation of the island for forestry purposes.

All this sort of nonsense is part of the price which has to be paid when an area suffers the blight which falls upon it following the designation of National Park being inflicted upon it. I believe *Peter Simple* once referred to it as 'statutory beauty.' 'Koms the Revolution and you'll all eat caviar.'

Not surprisingly, and rather wisely, the Freemans decided to go their own way. They had no great knowledge of wild-life when they settled on Ramsey, but they have developed a quickening interest with each passing season, as they have seen the spring and autumn migrations of so many interesting birds, and they have established wild-duck on the island's ponds, and an increas-ing number of pheasants. By constantly waging war on the rabbits, mainly through the use of ferrets, there is some indi-cation that success is being achieved, and the lovely wild flowers that have always bedecked the cliff-tops throughout the spring and summer are again a delight.

Now that the seal-ringing has been stopped, and the seals are left in peace, they are again breeding on the beach at the old landing place just below the house.

On the farm there are a hundred and twenty deer, and over two hundred breeding ewes, mostly of the Beulah speckle faced type, being crossed with Suffolk rams. Each year they are doing better, as the mainland dwellers who see them coming out have been quick to note.

When the Freemans came to Ramsey, the late Ivor Griffiths of Rhosson, a man wise in the ways of the islands, and whose father had been bailiff on Ramsey to the Williams of the Grove in the last century, gave them much useful advice. Amongst other things he impressed on them that trying to wrest a living from an island was different and that they would have to make their money where they could see the chance. So, not unnaturally, they have begun to build up a business of day visitors to what is a very fine nature reserve, although it has not been without difficulties.

On the jetty Alison has established a small shop to provide cups of tea and sandwiches for the daily visitors who are brought across in the Freeman's own launch,' the *Ramsey Pilot*, from St. Justinian's.

There is also the bungalow at Ysgubor, built before the first World War, and this is in constant demand during the season and provides another source of income by being let to weekly visitors.

The challenge of crossing Ramsey Sound still remains, but there are various ways in which life has been made easier. The acquisition of a radio telephone, for example, has changed their lives, removing some of the feeling of complete isolation, and facilitating day-to-day communication with the mainland.

They also have the benefit of the very comfortable house, completely re-built by the late K. P. Allpress. The central heating, however, was not a success, because of the voracious appetite of the solid fuel needed to heat the water. It is quite sufficient to have to hump coal for the Rayburn cooker in fertiliser bags from St Justinian's. The wood-burning stove was also found to consume too much drift-wood, which can be put to better use for carpentry and building, and it was therefore pulled out. There is a small gas powered refrigerator and another which can be switched on at night when the electric generator is operating. This is powered by diesel, which has to be shipped across in forty-five gallon drums.

Eggs, of course, are produced on the island, there are bees, vegetables are grown in the fertile garden and Alison bakes her own bread. But provision is not what it was in days of yore when people, and islanders in particular, also churned their own butter and salted their home-killed pigs. Indeed, Alison even gave up keeping a few goats to produce their own milk because there were not enough hours in the day, or days in the year, to anticipate and forestall their next attack on the trees or vegetable garden. Nowadays they can bring back fresh milk from a farm on the mainland, weather permitting, whenever they are over there and, of course, in between times, there is long-life milk to be had from the supermarket.

The word 'supermarket' did not exist in the vocabulary of the islanders of old, but now there is the fine new Tesco store in Haverfordwest. They do a 'big shop' once a month and then, in the autumn, ready for the winter, there is a really 'big shop' to stock up in preparation. To see a young couple pushing a dozen Tesco trolleys out to the car must give many folks cause to pause and ponder. They would perhaps pause and ponder a bit more if they also had to be involved in humping the contents across Ramsey Sound in an open boat.

The other mainland interest is the Freeman's own shop in St David's, looked after by a local lady, where they sell high class antique maps and views of Pembrokeshire and Wales. And there will soon have to be mainland interest in education for two growing boys. But no doubt things will happen to point the way just as they seem to have done all along the line to date.

I said earlier that change was written on all earthly things, and I also said in a note to one of the later editions *Cliffs of Freedom* that you cannot rewrite history.

What I have written thus far, therefore, I have written. That is history. At least, the events of which I have written are history, and I had recorded the story of the Freemans up to the autumn of 1985. Now, as there pages go to print, in the spring of 1987, the old wheel is turning again. Sad though it is to recall, I have all too frequently had occasion to spell out that, within the economy of the twentieth century, it is virutally impossible to make a living farming an off-shore island.

Apart from the dark days of the 1920's it is difficult to imagine when farmers have experienced worse time than the 1980's. As inflation rocketed in the 1970's the banks pushed money at farmers and encouraged them to borrow to the limit of the increasing paper value of their land. With land prices dropping the inevitable happened and, as the Common Market chickens start coming home to roost, it is with real apprehension that people in the rural community open their weekly papers to see which well-known farmer is the latest to be taken into receivership, or to have had his farm repossessed by Barclays or maybe some other bank. It has long been a maxim amongst farming people that a bank manager is a man who lends you an umbrella when the sun is shining and asks for it back when it starts to rain. Metaphorically, it is raining rather heavily on the farming community at the moment.

That very capable man, the late Bertie Griffiths of Carnwchwrn, knew exactly what he was doing in leaving Ramsey when he did. I wrote to him the *The Sounds Between,*' In 1947 he came back to the mainland for farm because he feared that farming would again be subjected to the same shameful betrayal as in the 1920's and if it was to be a question of a backs-to-the wall fight he wanted to be free of the encumberance of Ramsey Sound to impede him in his efforts.'

In the same book I also pointed out that, for some odd reason, it would appear that those who had survived and succeeded on the islands, even in earlier centuries, were those who had no foothold on the mainland. And the Freemans and a foothold on the mainland.

For the Freemans the time has come. Not, as I have written earlier in this chapter, there will soon have to be. The time has come when Griff has had to go to school. That has been the eternal difficulty facing islanders ever since schooling began.

There have been other difficulties, too. At the beginning of the 1986 'summer season', the Freemans lost their boat, the *Ramsey Pilot,* or at any rate had it so badly damaged that they lost the use of it pending extensive repair work. It was wretched luck, of course. But then, it is the sort of catastrophe which is always likely to happen to those who live on an island. There is always something. Rather like Will Fyffe's old music-hall song of the inebriated return home up the garden path, 'Two steps forward and three steps back.' Or was it the other way about, three forward and two back? What does it matter? The answer is the same. If it is as easy as all that, why are there so many islands all round our coast which have long since been abandoned?

Sad though it is to have to report, the Freemans can see the writing on the wall and, marvellous memories though they will have to take with them, they doubt whether they will be able to carry on much longer.

In *The Sounds Between* I made reference to the close relationship which for years had existed between Ramsey and the St David's lifeboat. I also referred to the loss of the lifeboat the *Gem*, together with three of her crew, in 1910 when she went to the aid of the Barnstaple ketch, *Democrat*, off the Bitches.

I wrote of this episode '. . . a dozen of the lifeboat crew and the three from the *Democrat* managed to save themselves and were rescued by local boatmen the following morning. Whenever this rescue is mentioned it invariably causes controversy in the area as to who did what and it is not therefore proposed in this instance to give any further details. Ample accounts and letters are available in the local press at various times since then for those who are interested. The official records give Sidney Mortimer, a local man, as having been awarded the Conspicuous Gallantry Medal by H.M. King George V and Silver Medal of the RNLI.'

I was fully aware of the controversy, but saw no point in dealing with it in any detail. Recently, however, a booklet has been published entitled *The Story of the St David's Lifeboats*. In the reference to the loss of the *Gem* the details given are very much the Sidney Mortimer version.

A distinguished seaman, Capt. S. R. (Jim) Arnold was particularly saddened that this myth should have been thus perpetuated. He did not mind too much that Sidney Mortimer, particularly in the eventide of his life, should be permitted a certain amount of latitude but, when his version became incorporated as fact in an official version of the St David's lifeboat story, Capt. Arnold felt it was time to put the record straight. He therefore wrote to the Hon. Secretary of the St. David's lifeboat and deposited at the Pembrokeshire Records Office a copy of his statement.

'The Gem Disaster and its Aftermath

The story of the *Gem* disaster as related in Hampson and Middleton's interesting little booklet, could in the main only have been written after recording Sidney Mortimer's subjective version of events on that fateful day. It is less than generous to dismiss in two sentences the efforts of the second boat which arrived on the scene a mere fifteen minutes after Mortimer, this despite the fulsome praise that is on record, given to both boats by the lifeboat committee on October 14th 1910, the day after the rescue had been effected.

Although it unfortunately resurrects old controversies it is necessary to see that historical justice is given to all participants, particularly to men who did not at any time posses that flamboyant locquacity, ever the hall-mark of Sidney Mortimer.

When the two Arnold brothers, then in Penarthur, heard of the *Gem* predicament, they proceeded at speed to Porthclais and demanded of Eleazar James that he give them his boat to participate in the rescue attempt. Sidney Mortimer had already left. James was reluctant to lend his boat much less to take part in any rescue attempt until conditions had improved. This resulted in an altercation which was both heated and public. The Arnold brothers were determined to take the boat with or without his consent. James eventually agreed to go and thereafter coxed the boat expertly and efficiently with Ivor and Adrian Arnold and two others, both named John Davies, obviously not brothers, making up the other four members of the boat.

While the rescue was being effected, fourteen and a half miles away in an E.S.E. direction the Dock Master at Milford docks went about his routine duties probably unaware of the drama unfolding in Ramsey Sound. One of his chores was to log prevailing weather twice a day. As the wind was off the land his records would be of significance.

Wednesday, 12 October, 1910:
A.M.—Wind moderate, North, squally, Barometer
    29.80 inches
P.M.—Nothing recorded.

Thursday, 13th October, 1910:
A.M.—Wind strong, N.E., squally, Barometer 30.00 inches
P.M.—Wind fresh E.N.E., Squally, Barometer 30.20 inches
This log abstract is presented here without further comment.

To return to the second boat; the Arnold brothers claimed that conditions were uncomfortable but not dangerous. As this second boat approached the Bitches, survivors on the rock seeing this second boat a mere quarter of an hour away decided, of their own volition, to wait, thus allowing both boats to share credit in the epic rescue. Subsequent history would show that this was the last thing Sidney Mortimer wanted. His claim that the second boat ran into difficulty on its return to Porthclais was dismissed with contempt by the Arnold brothers, and understandable feeling which such an untrue claim would amply merit.

It can be asked why was Eleazer James not suitably rewarded for sharing the rescue success. A person who had to be publicly bullied or coerced into taking part was hardly a candidate in 1910 for a bravery award. The five golden sovereigns each Arnold brother got was reward enough for them. An interesting footnote may be added. Adrian bought himself, what was then, an expensive clock with his £5. Seventy-five years later his son, Donald, had the clock repaired with the same firm of jewellers for £38!

There was a fourth member in Mortimer's boat, a shadowy character who has long been ignored. Can it be that like the Arnold brothers he felt that five gold sovereigns in the hand was wealth indeed? After all, the alternative was simply a recommendation for an award. Whatever the reason he is mentioned here to set yet another aspect of the record straight.

It would be remiss not to add the corollary to the *Gem* rescue. Mortimer at 18½ years was indeed made coxwain but it was soon made apparent to the R.N.L.I. that their confidence in one so young was misplaced. When on a duty call, the temporary boat, *Charlotte*, was being set down rapidly on to a lee-shore, Mortimer left the tiller, hid amidship and cried for his mother. Ivor Arnold took over the tiller, called for renewed effort and thus averted yet another pulling and sailing lifeboat disaster.

This incident must have filtered back to the lifeboat committee. Mortimer's only defence was to malign his crew. This incident was reported to the writer many times by both the Arnold brothers. Suffice it to say that in less than twelve months of being appointed coxwain Mortimer was dismissed. Perhaps the more charitable way of putting it was that in less than a year his resignation was accepted.

In Hampson and Middleton's booklet 'The Story of the St. David's Lifeboats' uncertainty creeps in as to who was coxwain in 1911. Page 30 would show that Mortimer was coxwain from 1910 to 1913, yet on page 15 Arnold was coxwain of the boat in the *Sarah MacDonald* incident of 1911. What is known is that Ivor Arnold relinquished command of the boat in 1918 when he went farming at Caerhedren Isaf where, incidentally, the writer was born. On returning to the St. David's area in 1923 he was again made coxwain and remained so until reaching retirement age in 1936. Once Mortimer on the other hand quit the service the break was final and complete.

It would be appropriate at this point to look back across the years at the characters of the participants. Sidney Mortimer, a born raconteur, was a larger than life figure. Romantic embellishment and hyperbole was a built-in characteristic. How could a young person displaying such gallantry one year be guilty of sheer fright bordering on terror the next? The advance of psychiatry since those far off days would see nothing inexplicable in such behaviour. Of the Arnold brothers, both retiring personalities bordering on shyness, it is inconceivable, reared as they were within the strict tenets of Calvinism, that they would fabricate and repeat an untrue story of Mortimer, leaving the tiller to crouch and whimper when disaster threatened. It is relevant that, having been previously corrected for inaccuracies, Mortimer did not again repeat them in print until both Arnold brothers had died.

Almost as a footnote one can conclude by adding that the writer, the younger son of Ivor Arnold, spent 44 years with ships and shipping, fifteen of which were spent in command, including command of the then largest containership in the world. His judgement and ability was rewarded by his being appointed Nautical Adviser to a then thriving Liverpool shipping company, to be the first shipmaster to be appointed to the Board. At the time of writing he is Deputy Chairman of the Milford Haven District Pilotage Authority. This is mentioned merely to show possible future readers that his critical judgement and objective assessment were not devoid of value to his peers. He served on many national and international maritime committees. He always found Mr. Mortimer a kindly charcter, who gave warmly of his friendship to people he liked. However, subjective reporting influenced by friendship is valuless to the historian; truth, however brutal its clarity, must prevail. Only thus can justice be awarded to all those involved in the maritime drama of that far off day.

The lifeboat secretary of St. David's may wish to keep this account on the files for historic reference. It may be of value to a trained historian of the future.

    S. R. (Jim) Arnold
      Master Mariner'

Chapter 6

Oil On The Water

The last time I visited Grassholm was in July 1980, and a glorious outing it was.

There is nothing about Grassholm as an island to call anyone to return there again and again as there is with the other, bigger islands, apart from the gannets, and they are something special.

The late Alastair Alpin MacGregor in his book, *An Island Here and There*, quoted a description of them.

'Above their sea-girt fortress they glide, translucent-winged, to fill the sky like a myriad giant snowflakes and occasionally transform the spectacle from magnificent to breath-taking as, with their six-foot wing span close-folded and streamlined for the kill, they plummet from a great height with the speed and certainty of an arrow to pierce the water in search of fish. Sometimes, too, they may even be seen nearer to land hunting amongst the porpoise-driven shoals and, when these magnificent birds are seen thus close, it is rarely long before the steady, sweeping roll of the porpoises disturbs the calm and sunlit sparkle of the blue ocean. The smell, however, is far less appealing. Unless a boat stands well off to windward the stench is wafted in all-pervading heaviness, whilst on the island, where there is this huge concentration of fish-eating birds, it is quite overpowering.'

That is the passage as quoted by MacGregor and, as he was quoting from my own writing in *The Sounds Between*, I see no point in either arguing with it or trying to improve it. It certainly is a fair description of the gannets as we saw them again that day in 1980.

We went from Dale in the Dale Sailing Company's boat, and it cost us £150 for twelve of us. At £12.50 per head it was marvellous value for money. I mention the figure because part of the purpose of this book is to bring the record up-to-date and, maybe a hundred years from now, people would like to know about these things. The figure of twelve passengers is also decreed by the

Board of Trade as being the maximum number allowed outside the smooth water limit.

Over the years I have organised many such trips for the benefit of friends and whenever such a trip was mooted, my wife's heart used to sink. I would be responsible for chartering the boat and would divide the charge by twelve to establish the going-rate per head. That much was always fairly easy. That was the theory. In practice it was rather different because some could not give an answer straight away and, the day before the appointed day, even assuming the weather looked favourable, there was nearly always somebody who would have to drop out at the last minute anyway. Then I would have to be looking round frantically trying to remember the names of friends who had said always to bear them in mind when such a trip was likely. In the end, I kept a list of such candidates. And I found it useful because, in the event of failure to make up the number, either I would have had to make up the deficit or face the embarrassment of explaining that it was going to cost more than I had said. Neither prospect appealed. That was why my wife's heart used to sink. It used to take quite a bit of organising.

I told in my book *Caldey* how my wife had died very suddenly and how I had remarried, so there is no point in re-telling that here. I, a widower, met my present wife on Caldey in the morning and proposed the same afternoon. Let that suffice. Our trip in 1980 was her first to the islands, apart from Caldey, and that, too, made it something special.

The instigator on that occasion was an old agricultural journalist friend, Denis Russell, who was anxious to arrange the trip for a few other friends. I was responsible for making up the number. We all met up after the Royal Show at Kenilworth, and there was never a hitch from first to last. Apart from the fact that Denis was sea-sick.

Normally, leaving from Dale, the programme would be to take a brief look at Skokholm in passing and then go on up to Skomer to drop anchor in South Haven for a picnic lunch. There can be few more delightful places on a hot, summer's day than to cruise close in under the great cliffs and to see the auks on the ledges and the kittiwakes with their nests clinging to the rock face. Truly it must have been one of the great spectacles of the world a century ago before oil pollution took its deadly toll. After a short while, with an engine ticking over whilst stationary, a slight oily film will be seen on the smooth surface of the water, and it is just an awful reminder of what even the most innocent of seafarers has been contributing, drip by deadly drip, towards the death toll of these lovely creatures. Then, after a look at the Wick, it would be due west to see the great gannet colony.

It is a remarkable sight aproaching Grassholm as it climbs steeply out of the water ahead. On the north, or starboard, slope there is just a thin line of white. Really speaking, you are looking at a cross-section of the gannetry. Once ashore, when the steep slope has been climbed, you look down on the island sloping the other way and there is this tightly-packed, seething mass of great white birds.

That day, early in July, just about all the eggs had hatched, most of the nests contained a young gannet, and the adult birds therefore stayed close. Apart from the stench, there is also the spectacle of the seaweed, and so much of the flotsam and jetsam thrown up by the sea, which the gannets bring home as nesting material. And these days that includes a high proportion of nylon line and netting. Man will surely have much for which to answer one day.

On the periphery at the point nearest to us was a young gannet whose life expectation had to be strictly limited. On this occasion one of the adult birds had brought home as nesting material the four-ringed plastic or nylon top, the original function of which would have been to hold together four tins of ale, lager or other such beverage, for the sustenance of those who, having consumed their contents, would scuttle the empty tins with the same reckless abandon as they would already have jetisoned the plastic top. The young gannet had emerged from the shell with its head through one of the rings and there he was, several weeks old, with the plastic firmly in place.

Whether I did the right thing or not I do not know, but I did it, for there was nothing else I could think to do. My wife produced a pair of scissors and, very quietly, I edged my way down to the bespangled younker and snipped away the impediment. So I saved the life of one young gannet, but whether I would have caused the loss of others I do not know. The disturbance as the birds on the nearest nests flapped and churned out of distance was, as I knew it would be, quite considerable. Within seconds a greater black backed gull swooped in to demolish an egg which had been left momentarily unattended, and I was glad to note that the egg was addle. I did not notice any other eggs being stolen, or see any chicks being trampled in the stampede, but it highlights the harm that can be done by the well-intentioned as well as by the unthinking. Whether the casters-away of debris would be concerned by what we saw that day I do not know, but would doubt it.

Another such trip as the one to which I have just been referring took place in the July of 1964, towards the end of the month. It is about the best time of all for seeing the sea-birds on the ledges, with the young ones ready to take to the water, and the adult birds preparing to go back to sea.

On this occasion the instigator was the late Guy Hains, a farming friend, who had enjoyed my book *Cliffs of Freedom*, and who had for some time been expressing an interest to go to see Skomer with his wife and two daughters. As usual, I made up the number from my list. Although Guy went to see Skomer it was the birds which fascinated him and his wife, Jean. Their interest grew and, as a result, they joined the West Wales Naturalists' Trust and became active with it. Guy was that sort of man. Where he was interested he was active. Much of my association with him had been through our activities, often turbulent, with the local branch of the National Farmers' Union.

In the October of 1978, Pembrokeshire people in general, and lovers of birds everywhere, learned with horror that a Greek oil tanker, the *Christos Bitas*, had struck the Hats and Barrels reef between Grassholm and the Smalls. Thousands of tons of light crude oil were spewed into the sea, but nobody could ever estimate how many thousands of sea-birds died horrible deaths as their oil-encased bodies were washed up round the coast.

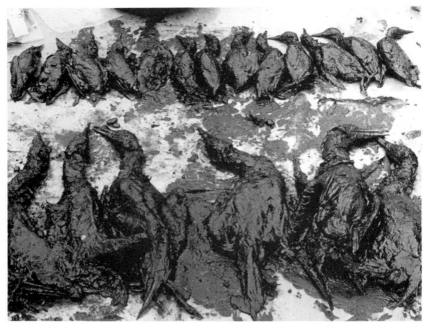

The price of oil.   Picture: Martin Cavaney.

Although the breeding season was over, and the birds and their young had left the ledges of the off-shore islands and the more inaccessible mainland cliffs, the disaster was so horrific that it seems hard to believe that it could have been even worse. It was, however, the height of the breeding season for the various colonies of Atlantic grey seals, and it was a pathetic and sickening sight to see the dead bodies of seal pups, their white fur smothered in oil, being washed ashore.

Guy and Jean Hains, of Lower House Farm, West Williamston, along with many other members of the West Wales Naturalists' Trust, turned out to do what they could to help by collecting and trying to clean some of the stricken birds. But the only place where anything could be done was at the bird hospital in New Quay, Cardigan, run by Mr and Mrs Alan Bryant. First of all the birds were taken to Lower House Farm, where make-shift

An oiled guillemot.
Picture: Martin Cavaney

arrangements achieved something, but the whole task was far beyond anything that was possible with such inadequate facilities.

It was following this that Guy and Jean gave the whole matter much thought and considered the possibility of converting an old farm-building. The building they had in mind was a former 17th century corn grist mill which had more recently been used for housing turkeys.

Converting old buildings was nothing new to them for, in the 1960's, they were something by way of pioneers in converting some of their obsolete farm buildings into three holiday cottages. Jean also knew something of birds, her mother having kept a number of cage-birds, when Jean was a girl in Birmingham before going to agricultural college. And after that she had done some nursing.

That same winter, in January 1979, conversion work began with the help of voluntary labour from members of the Trust, augmented by the efforts of young offenders putting in their time as part of their 'community service.' This was followed later with youths, who had been unable to find employment, working under the Government-sponsored community industries scheme.

Money, however, was needed for materials. Originally a loan of £1,500, which was subsequently repaid, was received from the Dyfed Wildlife Appeal. £3,000 was raised from voluntary contributions, with support from Councils, Rotary and Round Table. Then came a welcome boost with £1,000 from Texaco, and the other four big oil companies with refineries or terminals in the county followed suit with similar amounts. Not that they were in any way involved, in this particular case, in a disaster caused by the gross negligence of the captain of a foreign ship trying to take a short cut, with none of her navigational instruments in working order.

And, as Jean Hains is quick to point out, 'It's man has caused these problems, and at least it's a token that we can try to help to put it right. Every day we all use something connected with oil.'

The late Guy Hains (right) with Ron Elliott.

Thus was the Oiled Bird Centre at West Williamston established, and Jean Hains emphasises that everything is done on a completely voluntary basis and the the whole effort is very much that of the re-named West Wales Trust for Nature Conservation, rather than personal, although her own contribution is considerable, and she is, in fact, Honorary Warden.

The Trust were given a forty-year lease on the building and pay a peppercorn rent.

'It started as a dream' Jean says, 'and it became a reality. Every bird that comes here is a potential dead bird. Without being big-headed, our recovery rate is very good. And when birds die, at least they can die with a bit of dignity instead of in agony.'

To learn something of the technique herself she went to Alan and Jean Bryant at New Quay for a couple of days and cannot speak too highly of all the help and encouragement they gave.

It takes two people anything from an hour to an hour-and-a-half to clean a bird, with one holding the bird and one washing.

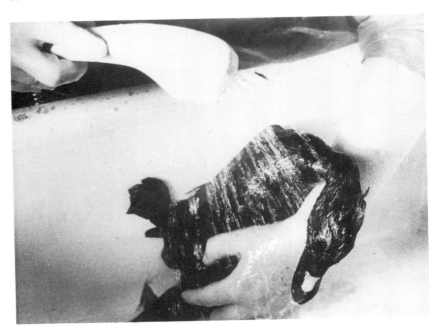

Glad to be better and taking nourishment. Share and share alike.

'It's important,' Jean says, 'to use a detergent which has been specially tested for us and which contains no barriers. If not, a residue is left on the feathers, and although it looks clean it will never become waterproof.'

After being thoroughly rinsed, the birds are placed in a pen with infra-red heat until their feathers are dry. Then they are moved to a preening area for two days before being moved to the pool where it can be seen whether they are ready to be returned to the sea. The works is, of course, tedious and time-consuming, and even those who pick up the technique quickly need to be constantly on their guard and continue to pay attention to detail.

Sadly, Guy died, after a long illness, in 1985. He had been an enthusiastic worker in many causes. But he lived to see something of which he was very proud come to fruition. In December 1981 the Centre received one of the Prince of Wales awards for contributions to the environment, and it continues in good hands with the enthusiasm of dedicated people and a sound committee of management.

Ron Elliott receives the Prince of Wales Award.

One of them, Ron Elliott, acts as Recorder, and his figures show that, since the Centre came into being, they have already, up to the end of 1985, treated 1,460 birds. The records also show that, of all the birds received, something like sixty percent have eventually been released.

Of the birds brought in for treatment no fewer than 517 have been shearwaters. There have been eighty razorbills, eight-five guillemots and thirty-two gannets. Surprisingly, perhaps, there have only been four puffins. Altogether no fewer than eight-two individual species of birds have been brought in.

British Trust for Ornithology rings are fitted to birds before they are released but, as yet, there has been little to show by way of recoveries. This is perhaps understandable when it is re-membered that the majority of sea-birds would tend to die at sea.

Apart from a guillemot picked up after a few months the only recovery has been a kittiwake which was picked up at Amroth in

February 1982. It was heavily oiled on the breast, feet and legs, and around the top of the beak. It was washed four days later and, a fortnight after that, on March 4th, it was released from Giltar Point, near Tenby. On June 24th, 1985, it was picked up freshly shot in Greenland.

'What sort of mentality would want to shoot such a beautiful bird,' Jean Hains says, 'I just can't imagine. But this three-and-a-half year span and the distance travelled by this bird give us great hope and encouragement to keep up our high standard and to endeavour to keep on improving.'

Well, there it is. Not strictly islands, but arising from a visit to them, and very much related to them when we remember that most of the oiled sea-birds brought there will have been born on one or other of the lovely islands round Pembrokeshire's lovely coast. Not quite as lovely since the coming of the oil refineries and

Mrs. Jean Hains.

their attendant power station, of course, all of which made nonsense of the so-called National Park designation. But there are still people sufficiently muddle-headed to believe that a National Park is something to do with beauty and conservation rather than money and jobs for the boys.

Not that the oil refineries brought any prosperity to the area. And now they show signs of moving out with the prospect of leaving one more derelict area behind them. What was even more galling to Pembrokeshire motorists was the fact that petrol consistently remained a couple of pence a gallon dearer in the west than anywhere further east.

I first made reference to the nonsense, which was made of the so-called National Park designation with the coming of oil to Pembrokeshire, in *Cliffs of Freedom*. I also referred to the nonsense of the attitude of the West Wales Field Society towards the annual collecting of gulls' eggs on Skomer by the local people from Marloes. The Society put a stop to this collecting and now, as these pages go to the printers, there is great publicity being given to the fact that the position is now, more than quarter of a century later, so out of control on Skomer that the gulls are having to be poisoned. Talk about the sins of the fathers!

Still, the operation has received the blessing of the National Park's Planning Officer, if you have ever heard of anything so farcical. Few people suspected that he was an authority on ornithology as well. But, as far as the gulls are concerned, if what the worst that so-called planning has done for Pembrokeshire is anything to go by, it will still need some real countrymen to be called in to tell them how many beans make five.

Chapter 7

Caldey

Having written two books on Caldey, and the more recent of them having been published as recently as the spring of 1984, there is not so very much to record to bring the story up-to-date, but there are a few errors to be corrected. I am glad to say that they are not serious.

In my book *Caldey* I referred to the possibility of a railway which was reputed to have run from the top of High Cliff quarry for carrying the stones from which the monastery was built. I had not, however, been able to find anyone who could remember it. Once again it was a question of not happening to ask the right person. I discovered, after the book was published, that Miss Bridie Cummins remembered it quite well.

I made another small mistake in the order of those who ran the old Priory guest house. It was Dom Wilfred Upson's sister who ran it first, and then the McHardy girls, Veronica and Mary, took over and built it up before the Misses Grossé, aunts of one of the Chimay monks who came over in 1930, were brought in.

Perhaps a more serious mistake was my failure to identify the Tenby draper who used to go over to conduct services in the church on Caldey during the last century. It was, in fact, Stephen Davies, who founded the family business of that name in Tenby. Time was when there were letters which told of his endeavours in this sphere, but these have now been lost.

In *Caldey* I told how James Hawksley bought the island in 1867 and brought with him a young man, John King, who had been his right-hand man on his farm at Navistock in Essex. John King lodged with the farm bailiff on Caldey, Benjamin Oriel, and, in 1872, married Benjamin's daughter, Sarah.

Of the many interesting and delightful letters I have received since *Caldey* was published, one was from a descendant of John King, Miss Eira King, who said, 'We have been to Navistock, where

John King was born, and have been to the church several times, where he sang in the choir and there are gravestones to his parents and grand-parents. We have often thought, as we travelled the road away from the church and looked over the fields, about John King and Mr Hawksley travelling the same road in 1867 on their way to Caldey, and I have been told how Sarah and her friend were watching the boat coming to Caldey bringing some strangers with Mr Hawksley and Sarah said 'I'll have the fair one'—and she did!! So, you were not the first to make up your mind quickly on Caldey!'

(I had recounted in *Caldey* how I had met my wife there in the morning and proposed the same afternoon.).

Miss King also told me how, when they were bringing David Oriel back from Aberbeeg to be buried in Tenby, the hearse broke down at Sennybridge and the coffin had to be transferred to a taxi. It must have been an interesting, even if unusual, cortege.

To me, however, the most interesting details to come to light have been concerning the love-life of Cabot Kynaston who dominated life on Caldey for the bigger part of the nineteenth century. Up to the time *Caldey* was published I had only been able to say that Cabot, 'would have been born about 1792.' I have since discovered that he was born on July 21st 1792 and that he and his sister and three brothers were baptised together on January 26th 1796 at St Mary's church, Pembroke. I also related how between the years 1814 and 1822, Martha Jenkins of Caldey bore Cabot no fewer than six daughters before they subsequently married by licence at Manorbier church in 1833.

A boy, William Kynaston, died on Caldey in May 1840 at the age of seventeen and was given as Cabot's son. This led to the conjecture that Cabot was already married and thereby unable to marry Martha. I still think this was a strong possibility. However, I also explained that before the *Poor Law Amendment Act* of 1834, where an unmarried mother claimed that a particular man was the father of her child, the onus was on the man to prove otherwise if he wished to deny parentage. If the mother on oath charged a man with paternity, a magistrate could commit him until he gave security either to maintain the child or to appear at quarter sessions to dispute the fact. Hence it is not at all unusual in church registers of the day to find such entries as Reputed Father, Claimed child of, and so on.

Many a country squire was fair game for such tactics, and it was not unknown for them to pay up without bothering to argue. The law, however, was soon to be changed with a vengeance, with the onus now being placed on an often helpless girl to prove parentage.

Since *Caldey* was published I have had my attention drawn to two rather interesting entries in the Jeffreston parish church register. They were,

> 1821, Dec 23rd Henry reputed sone of Cabot Kynaston and Mary James, Caldey, baptised.
> 1822, June 2nd William reputed son of Cabot Kynaston and Phoebe James, Caldey, baptised.

There were people working on Caldey from the Jeffreston area, as there were from many of the neighbouring villages. Could the girls have gone home to have their babies and named Cabot as being 'fair game'? Or was William really Cabot's son, to be recognised in due course, and could he have been the William Kynaston who died in 1840 aged seventeen? There are still people who come to this area in the summer and say, 'What on earth do people find to do here in the winter?' These days they even have television as well.

For television, of course, it is necessary to have electricity, and mains electricity came to Caldey, courtesy South Wales Electricity Board via a submarine cable, in 1965. I was writing for the lately lamented, rather undistinguished *Farm News* at the time and went over to Caldey at the behest of S.W.E.B., along with some journalistic colleagues, to cover the great occasion. I like to think I did justice to it, but concluded my report with a personal note (I was of sufficient standing with the paper to be permitted this small liberty from time to time.) I wrote,

'I asked Father Stephen whether they intended to maintain the existing plant as some sort of emergency reserve, after they were connected to the mains, in case of power cuts.

Officials of the South Wales Electricity Board, however, immediately stressed that there had only been two power cuts since the bad winter of 1962-3. Asked what had happened in Carmarthen the previous evening they explained that that was only a break-down.

The thought that a break-down didn't really count was greeted with great good humour by those present. I must admit I thought it was rather a good joke myself, but when I recounted it on coming home late that night nobody connected with our establishment seemed to see the funny side of it.

It turned out that there had been a break-down from 4-0 P.M. until 8.30 P.M. which had seriously interfered with milking routine, and the position had been further aggravated by the fact that the telephone was out of order.

In the face of which I could only comment, 'Isn't it a good job we don't have to farm on an island, and let us be thankful it was just a break-down and not a power cut'.'

There are many ways in which life on an island can take its toll. Reuben Codd, of Skomer, dropped dead of a heart attack at the the age of sixty-eight. Br Thomas, of Caldey, dropped dead of a heart attack at the age of fifty-seven. Both of them were big, strong men, and both of them, in earlier years, had strained their hearts whilst wrestling single-handed with their boats in rough seas.

At the time of writing *Caldey* I told how, following the resignation of Dom James Wickstead as Abbot, authority reverted, under Canon Law, to the mother house at Chimay. The Abbot of Chimay, Dom Guerric Baudet, appointed Fr Robert O'Brien as Superior *ad nutum*. In due course, when affairs seemed to be going along satisfactorily, an election was again authorised, and Fr Robert was elected the second Abbot of Caldey which again became an Abbey in its own right.

The abbatial blessing took place in June, 1984. My wife and I were privileged to be invited across to the island for the occasion and the service, conducted by Bishop James Hannigan, of Menevia, was moving and memorable. It was followed by the sort

The Abbatial blessing 1984.

of party in the lounge of the old abbatial quarters at which Caldey seems to excel.

Where there is a community, even on an island, changes are always taking place. Eventually the chocolate making became too much for Br John, and Fr Bertrand, a monk who had been 'borrowed' from Saint Sixte monastery in Belgium, took over for a while. When he left, the job was taken over by Frank Miller, a young man with a farming background, who had married Teresa Farrell. Her mother, Jill, has been associated with Caldey for some time and Teresa, who also helps in the shops on the island, will no doubt, find her qualifications as a nurse being put to good use.

Another interesting development has been through the Friends of Caldey. One of their number, Jim Purchase, was so attracted by the place that he and his wife, Ann, have gone to live there, with Jim now being the island handyman. His services are particularly valuable when organising the efforts of various groups of Friends of Caldey.

Caldey chocolate.   Caldey 'handyman'
Frank Miller and his wife Teresa.   Jim Purchase and his wife Ann.

There has been change, too, in the case of the splendid little primary school on the island, with the teacher, Audrey Robinson, taking early retirement and being replaced by Bryn Matthews, a married man with a grown-up family.

Whilst all these have been talking points amongst the island community, nothing was quite as exciting as the arrival of the fire engine. It was supplied by the county fire authority and delivered by Chinook helicopter.

Caldey's new school-master, Bryn Matthews, (right) visiting the island to meet the children and some of the parents in June 1986. Retiring schoolmistress Audrey Robinson front left.

There was excitement, too, when Caldey raised a cricket team to play Skomer, where the new warden, Stephen Sutcliffe, is a keen cricketer and formerly had close associations with Caldey. In the middle of a miserable summer, the August Saturday of the match was beautiful and the sea was calm. The Caldey contingent went by 'bus from Tenby, crossed to Skomer from Martinshaven, and a good time was had by all.

In a limited over encounter Caldey, batting first, were all out for 64. Skomer won in the last over by three wickets. As befitted an accountant, Peter Muxworthy returned the best figures for Caldey, taking 3 for 5 and making top score of 12. One ball was lost down a rabbit hole. Future archaeologists may find this information useful. The date was August 9th 1986.

The Caldey fire-engine being delivered by helicopter.
Picture: David Philippart.

For the beneift of the children Fr. Robert plays fireman for the day.
Picture: David Philippart.

The Caldey fire brigade.

The Caldey cricket squad on Skomer 1986.

Archaeologists, as well as many others, will also be pleased to know that restoration work is now under way on the old Priory, some parts of which had become unsafe. The work has been made possible with the help of a fifty percent grant from CADW.

More recently still, a shadow was cast over the island by the death, after a short illness, of the caldey farm manager, Peter Cummins, at the age of sixty-one. He had been born on the island and there was nowhere else he would have wished to end his days. A man of great Christian gentleness and kindness, it will be a long time before the island will again be quite the same for the many who respected and had a deep affection for him.

Normally, there would have been little more to write about Caldey to bring the details up-to-date, except that in the summer of 1985 I became involved rather unexpectedly. The guest-master was in hospital, and there was no knowing exactly when he could be expected back. One of his duties was to do the conducted tour of the monastery twice a day and, with a shortage of monks, this was one extra burden on the Community. After some discussion between the Abbot and the Prior it was arranged that, once the holiday season started, I would go across every day to act as guide. The only proviso I made was that I could not be available on certain religious festivals, such as when Glamorgan were playing cricket at Swansea. I also included the one game at Neath, and was so glad I did because I was there on that memorable day when Javed Miandad and Younis Ahmed (two good Welsh names) put on over three hundred runs for the fourth wicket in an unbroken partnership against the Australians and all sorts of records went by the board. In the event, my stint began in May and lasted until the end of August. It was a great privilege to have been entrusted with such a responsibility, and it was an experience I would not have missed for anything.

Suffering considerably from arthritis I found that there were some difficulties. As often as not, if the boat went from Tenby harbour in the morning, it would mean disembarking on the Castle beach on returning in the afternoon, followed by a long slog' up across the soft sand. Sometimes it was the other way round, with a slow crawl down across the soft sand, if the tide was out in

Graham Baxter and Allan Thomas renovating the old Priory.

the morning. Getting on and off the boats was not easy. The harbour-master was very helpful in ensuring that there was a place for me to park my car on the harbour, and the boatmen were all marvellous. I am of a generation who played rugby with the fathers and uncles of some of them. It was a salutary thought that some of these wizened old salts almost certainly regarded me as a decrepit old gentleman.

Normally the excursion would have involved a walk from the jetty on the island up to the monastery and a walk back again in the afternoon. Fr Stephen, however, who is responsible for the control of visitors to the island, and who would himself have had to conduct some of the tours had I not been available, ensured that I did not lack for transport in one or other of the assorted island vehicles which menace the well-being of passengers and pedestrians alike. They are subject neither to tax requirements nor M.O.T. tests. Sometimes when Fr Stephen was not there himself, my chauffeur would be the late Br Thomas's charming niece, Clare, or else students, who intend to become priests, and who help out in the tea-rooms during their summer holiday. Their attitude to life generally gave me the impression that the future of the Catholic Faith is in good hands.

As the first day of August approached, all the talk on the mainland was of the status symbol of acquiring a C registration motor car. That day on the jetty at Caldey I was met by a mini pick-up, which many would have described as a clapped-out abomination, with a big white sticker on the back, 'C REG'. I have ridden in many better vehicles, but never more gratefully. Now and again I went on the box at the back of Blackie's tractor.

I soon realised that I was privileged in other ways, too. I was a worker on the island. Not merely any longer a visitor who had also happened to write a couple of books about the place. But a worker. A member of a very select outfit.

The season opened and the Pool boats started to run on a Monday in May. It was perhaps another of those little instances in life where, if we trouble to look, we can see how God looks after us far better than we know or deserve. It so happened that on that Monday the local branch of the N.F.U., of which I am a long-serving member, had arranged a trip to Caldey, and the group-secretary, quite naturally, was looking to me to act as the official guide. So, as it turned out, my first party to be conducted round the monastery consisted of two or three visitors, plus twenty or so of my fellow N.F.U. members whom I had known for years.

This in itself was rather disconcerting. It was even more disconcerting when it came to question time afterwards to find one member, 'just to make it more interesting,' bombarding me with quite aggressive questions as to what the monks thought they were achieving, and what would be the commercial possibilities if they ever had to admit defeat, and why not exploit the island with all its holiday potential. It was an excellent grounding for me in the task which was to come during the ensuing summer months. At the end of it, however, I was greatly encouraged to hear one of the members, a life-long nonconformist, say, 'Now look here, boss. Those men in there are doing far more good for us by their prayers than all the developers exploiting the so-called National Park over there on the mainland, for just look across and see what's happened to it.'

I had quite a few such contentious customers to contend with before the season was finished but, unlike the tongue-in-cheek N.F.U. member, they were in real earnest. The N.F.U. episode, however, made me realise not only that I would have to do my homework, but also that there was much sympathy with the monks' aim in life.

Let me say, right at the outset, that of all the people who came on the tours, more than ninety percent of them were really interested and most appreciative. Several asked was there a contribution box, and I could only direct their attention to any boxes there may be at the church doors. One man, however, insisted on giving me a ten pound note for the monks. Some expressed great interest in the Friends of Caldey, the organisation of voluteers who come to the island in groups of about half-a-dozen, for a week or so a year, to give what help they can by way of repairs and maintenance.

Basically, where there was ignorance, it was because people don't have the faintest idea of what monasticism is about and, coming to the island for the first time with preconceived ideas, some of which are very odd indeed, they are almost offended when things are not in the least what they expect them to be.

Amongst a company of more than a hundred on one tour one gentleman of a particularly enquiring turn of mind waxed extremely disputatious about everything as far as I could make out from the rule of silence to the infallability of the Pope. When I had answered all his questions and arguments, courteously, and presumably entirely to his dissatisfaction, he said, 'The trouble with you Catholics is that . . .'

'Now wait a minute,' I said. 'Don't misunderstand me. I'm not a Catholic. I'm a staunch nonconformist.'

I regret to say, human nature being what it is, that there is something rather satisfying about seeing such characters floundering and gasping for air like a grounded goldfish.

Such people, of course, are rarely convinced. As Samuel Butler wrote in the seventeenth century. 'He that complies against his will, is of the same opinion still.' And man changes but little. But there is always the hope and the possibility that those who ask no questions, but listen with an open mind, might just find some small enlightenment on points which were previously rather obscure.

I have already said that the vast majority of the people were interested and appreciative. Unfortunately, human nature once more being what it is, it is the others who create the talking point when it comes time to report on the day's doings and you are asked, 'Any daft questions today?'

As a former journalistic colleague and good friend of mine, the late Stanley Baker, once wrote, 'When I say that wickedness is news and virtue is not, I am really affirming my faith in humanity for, since this is demonstrably the case, it must follow that wickedness is rarer than virtue.'

For wickedness, substitute stupidity, and the same truth applies. So can we remember this, in all fairness to the majority, bless their hearts, when I recall some of the other more memorable encounters?

It is only gentlemen who are allowed in the monastery, but ladies would also assemble at the starting point outside the main door, and there I would give a talk for ten minutes or so for the benefit of the ladies, and this usually seemed to be appreciated. I always considered this one to be the biggest hurdle because, in addition to the ladies, there was always likely to be a fair number of children and babes-in-arms. When some of the assembled gathering had satisfied their curiosity, and heard enough, they were likely to hold a committee meeting, not always *sotto voce*, decide it was not for them, and wander off licking their ice-creams. Unless, of course, there were napkins to be changed and bottoms to be powdered first of all. Sitting on the grass outside the monastery front door seemed to have been recognised as a suitable place for this performance, and my opening remarks also seemed to be regarded as a suitable time.

Before each tour I would go into the sacristy and peep through the window to see what the competition was likely to be. Rather like a stage performer peeping through curtains before the show to see what 'the house' is like.

Sometimes a child would start squalling and one of the parents would, very sensibly and quietly, take it away. Only once did I give up the unequal fight and say 'I can't compete with this' and say to the men, as I believe characters say in certain films on television, 'Let's go.'

One formidable trial was the Caldey camera. This trinket is sold for the benefit of small children and contains about ten colour slides. The child looks into the viewer, clicks, and up comes another slide with a pretty picture of the island. Maybe I am unduly sensitive about these things, but you try talking to more than a hundred people with half-a-dozen of these click, click, clickers pointed at you and clicking merrily away right under your nose. There were other diversions, too, but I shall not enumerate them. Suffice it for me to say that I finished the season more than ever convinced there is nothing much wrong with the majority of naughty children which could not be cured by giving either the father or the mother, or both, a good hiding. There is also the question of how much of this fractious behaviour is caused by the additives in the trash food of our present generation. But, here again, let me hasten to say, most of the children were a delight, and many of the boys asked some good questions in the enclosure afterwards.

On one notable occasion a lady was there with a reasonably behaved dog on a lead. Until the cook's tabby cat also decided to take an interest in the proceedings. But that sort of thing is an occupational hazard. Like the sporadic jet aeroplanes zooming in over the island. You can't compete with those either.

Stories amongst the islanders are legion concerning the daft questions people ask and the comments they make. Over the years I had regarded many of these stories as slightly suspect, far fetched or apocryphal, but after one season's close contact and personal experience, I am willing to believe anything. I finished up some days feeling like the guide to the National gallery who finally said to one contentious young customer, 'I'm not here to educate you, sir. I'm here to stop you nicking anything.'

Having finished the introductory talk from the steps outside the main door, the men were admitted to the cloisters. They were not taken into church because, apart from the cleaning necessitated by the trampling and shuffling of so many feet, the church is readily accessible from the outside anyway. A few words to start, then along the cloisters to the beautiful refectory, some more brief explanation, back to the cloisters, an explanation of the Stations of the Cross, which are the scenes of the last hours of Our Lord's agony all the way from his condemnation to Calvary, and then out into the monastic enclosure for a final session. Within reason, the idea is to move the crowd through the monastery as quickly as possible. This ensures that the inquisitive are given less time to poke and pry into things and places which are of no concern to them.

Out in the enclosure there is a chance to relax. First of all comes a brief explanation of the stages in which the various buildings developed. This includes pointing out the high Abbot's Tower built by Aelred Carlyle who laid claim to the title, Lord of the Manor of Caldey, and who thought it would be a good idea to have this tower so that he could climb to the top of it and look out over his domain. Having explained this very carefully, the first question I was asked on one occassion was, 'Is that tower the lighthouse?'

Yes, after this session came the questions.

Most of the questions were sensible and intelligent concerning the history of the island and monastic life. The answers to all these questions will be found in one or other of my books *Total Community* or *Caldey*, so there is no point in belabouring them again here. On the odd occasion I would be asked a question where I could not be sure of the facts, and then I would have to say so and offer a qualified answer. Afterwards, of course, I would ask one of the monks so that, by the end of the season, I knew rather more than when I started.

'Why do these monks have women in the dining room with them then if there's no women allowed in the monastery? Why is that then?'

'Women? Do they? I didn't know.'

'Aye, they do. I seen their mugs on the tables in there with their names on 'em. Margaret and Rosemary and Doris.'

'Oh, I see. Ah yes. Well, the monks sell these mugs down in the shop in the village. And some of them are seconds or slightly faulty. So, rather than throw them out they have them up to the monastery for their own use.'

How I wished that all of the less expected questions could have been so easy to answer.

One question was not so much a question as a statement of fact.

'These monks here now came here from Kidwelly.'

'Did they?'

'Yes, they did. From Kidwelly.'

'I don't think so.'

'Who did come here from Kidwelly then?'

'Well, I wouldn't know about that. It could have been anybody. And I can assure you no monks I've ever heard of came here from Kidwelly. Are you thinking of Whitland or Margam? There were famous monasteries there. But that was way back in the Middle Ages and I'm not any sort of authority on that side of it. But the

Reverend David Williams is, and he's written a number of books
on the subject which you may like to read.'

'No, not the Middle Ages. And not Whitland nor Margam. This
lot here now. Came from Kidwelly.'

'No, I think you'll find they came from Chimay in Belgium.'

'No it wasn't. It was Kidwelly.'

'Oh. Where did you read that?'

'I didn't read it. There was a man in the pub last week saying
about it. He knew all about them. He did say they came from
Kidwelly.'

'Well, next time you see him will you give him my compliments
and tell him he's talking a load of cobblers.'

'Is he?'

'Yes, he is.'

'Right. I'll tell him. But who did come from Kidwelly?'

'Oh, I don't know anything about Kidwelly. I only know about
Caldey.'

For the most part I was deeply conscious of the fact that I was
representing real men of God whose lives had been self-sacrific-
ingly devoted to their fellow men through prayer and self-denial,
and I tried to speak and conduct myself accordingly. But just once
in a while, as on the above occasion, I permitted myself the luxury
of saying just what I felt like saying. No monk, of course, could
have talked like that but, knowing some of them as I do, I have a
fair idea that they would often have felt like it.

'If these monks are shut away like this why do they have
telephones and electricity and all that sort of thing then? All these
modern things.'

'Ah, yes. Good question. Would you suggest that they also sell
their tractors, have the electricity cut off and go back to humping
coal up from the beach? And whilst they're at it would you also
suggest that instead of using matches they rub two sticks
together?'

No answer.

Then came Harry Worth. Or, if not Mr Worth himself, certainly
a close relation. Many and varied were the questions he asked.

Years ago, before the bay, which is now known as the Common, silted up, the sea used to come right up to the cottages in the village, and they were known as the cottages on the beach. The parish church, now known as St David's, was originally dedicated to the Virgin Mary and was known as the church of Our Lady on the Sea Shore. Here, for many years now, the islanders, monks and villagers, have been buried. And since women live on the island they, too, when the time comes, are buried in the island grave-yard.

It could just be that it was not one of my better days but, eventually, Mr. Worth said, 'Now could you tell me, please, for I really would like to know! Why did they bury those ladies in that cemetry out there?'

And, I regret to say, that, without thinking, I said, 'Because they'd died I suppose.'

Then I realised my answer could have sounded a little unkind and I went on to explain. Oddly enough, it gave rise to another question.

'Is it right that a Cistercian monk has to dig his own grave before he dies?'

That was one which really caught me unawares, and I had to admit that I just did not have a clue as to the answer, or even as to why the question had been asked.

As always, when the opportunity arose, I referred the question to higher authority.

I think I caught Fr Stephen, the Prior and Procurator, at the end of a particularly harassing day in the tea-rooms, and he said, 'Oh yes. I've been digging my own grave down here for years.'

The Abbot, when I found him, was in facetious mood and said, 'Was nobody after telling you about Brother Patrick then?'

A monastery is not normally the sort of place to expect an Irish joke.

Apparently, when Brother Patrick was professed, they told him he would have to dig his own grave before he died.

'All right' says he. 'I'll do that' says he. 'I'll dig six inches every Saturday morning.'

'And Brother Patrick will be eighty-six next spring.'

Fr Cyril, Novice Master, and a former Abbot of the Abbey at Mount St Bernard, provided the answer.

In the old days there were many more monks in the monasteries than there are today, so it was the custom always to have a grave ready. Furthermore, the grave-yards were part of the enclosure, so that the monks spent time in them during their hours of contemplation. On Caldey the grave-yard is outside the enclosure. But then, Caldey has always been just that little bit different.

Occasionally someone would demand to know what right did these men have to waste their lives shut off from the world. The answer to this question, like so many of the others, will also be found in *Total Community*. It was a question I was always happy to be asked because it is something about which I feel strongly.

One day, however, a man stayed behind for a personal chat, as some of them would quite often do, and he was on the same theme. I answered all his questions and, eventually, said to him, 'You have no Christian conviction, I suppose?'

'Oh no,' he said. 'None at all.'

This had been obvious from the start. So I then went on to offer the opinion that we all liked to think that our own work was important but that it was just as well we did not all want to do the same thing. Most of my life, for example, was in farming, but it was just as well everybody did not want to be farmers otherwise there would be nobody to make tractors for us to plough the fields. Equally it would be no good if everybody wanted to make tractors otherwise there would be nobody to use them. Some people would say that only doctors are indispensible to society, but others would point to the overcrowded hospitals and waiting rooms at doctors' surgeries to argue that doctors are the world's greatest failures. And I followed this up by asking, 'What do you do for a living?'

'Oh,' he said, 'I'm in computers.' The sad part was that he sounded really pleased with himself. So, ignoring their benefits and the marvellous achievements they make possible, and just for the sake of being awkward, as we say in Pembrokeshire, I said, 'Well, look at that! Computers! Can you think of anything more useless? Creating unemployment. Sending the wrong bills to the wrong people until some of them commit suicide. Trying to reduce people to a nation of automatons. But never mind, friend. I'm a great believer in the power of prayer and don't under-estimate it. 'More things are wrought by prayer than this world dreams of.' So I'll pray for you. And I'll pray for you that one day by God's grace you'll see the light and go out and do something useful like digging a garden.'

But I don't think he was impressed.

There was a much happier story one day when a gentleman stayed behind and gave me a purse which he and his wife had found on the floor of the old Priory. There was no name or anything in it other than forty odd pounds. The gentleman was the rector of Earl Shilton in Leicestershire. And we have already become familiar with Earl Shilton in these pages because it was there that Maud Fulshaw, (formerly Maud Davies of Skomer) went to live, and where she carved the pulpit of the church.

It turned out that the purse belonged to a girl from Birmingham and I travelled back to Tenby on the boat with her and her boyfriend.

Oddly enough, a few days previously, I had been asked why the Catholics lit candles in church. I said there was no particular reason as far as I knew except that Christ was the Light of the World. Apart from that it was probably just that they felt they wanted to do it by way of a small offering. Just that and no more.

So I asked this girl how she had come to drop her purse in the old Priory and she said she had put it down in order to light a candle. So I asked her was she a Catholic and she said, oh no, she was nothing at all. She was from Birmingham and she didn't go anywhere and they never had scripture in the schools or anything like that. So then I asked her why she had been lighting a candle, and she said, 'Oh I just saw them and I felt I just wanted to light one.'

Then we talked some more. The following evening it was the Harvest festival in our little chapel in Amroth and this young couple came.

Who knows? Who knows?

After writing this chapter I sent the first draft to Fr Stephen who offered a further coment. He said,

'Concerning lighting a candle. When I became a Catholic I, quite gratuitously, assumed that it was one of those practices of Italian origin safely to be ignored. If not superstitious at least of no importance. With age and, perhaps, more perception I now recognise it to be of value for many reasons—I light them myself.

Its value is symbolic, in the main. As you say, it is a demonstration of faith in Christ as the light of the world. But more than that, it symbolises the intentions and desires of the one lighting the candle.

It signifies the prayers, hopes and wishes, of the person: that, although they are no longer there in the church, their heart remains unchanged (to give themselves to God), a kind of substitute for their actual presence. It is a small gift to God, to burn through in his honour, simply to glorify him. It symbolises the gift of the donor of himself or herself to God. It bears testimony to the prayer they have made, whether of praise or petition. It has, as I have found, an extraordinary side effect of giving peace and calm—perhaps the sight of the flame burning motionless and unhurried? Anyhow, a few thoughts.

It is only in the last ten to fifteen years that I have come to realise the profound importance of symbols, how they permeate the whole of our Christian faith and worship, how the material symbolises, transmits and communicates the spiritual.'

Amidst all this activity and general good fellowship there was also the sadness, for in July the time came for the oldest member of the Community, Fr Anselm, to be called away to higher realms and I felt a certain personal loss. When my first wife died very suddenly—in fact, I found her dead on the floor half-an-hour after leaving her in good health—and I 'phoned Caldey to ask them for their prayers, it was Fr Anselm who answered the 'phone. His concern was great and the lovely letter which he wrote to me is one of many I treasure. Subsequently, when I met my present wife on Caldey and proposed to her, Fr Anselm was one of the first to be taken into our confidence.

Up to the time he had started to fail he had been guest-master in the Abbey guest-quarters where, for some years, although it is not so now, ladies were also sometimes accommodated. Not only was he a great raconteur and wit but also, like all the monks I have ever known, had a great sense of humour. Amongst other things he loved the Stanley Holloway monlogues which I would sometimes do for him over a cup of coffee after breakfast. A particular favourite with him was that epic of the Ramsbottom family crossing Runcorn ferry at 'tuppence per person per trip.'

He became very confused towards the end and one day, a week or so before he died, I went in to sit with him. When I went in I sat by the bed and said, 'It's Roscoe here Father,' but there was little response. I just sat there and he said nothing. Then, after a little while, he smiled and in his rich deep voice, chuckled quietly, 'Tuppence per person per trip.'

Father Anselm spent the last months of his life, and died, in the new infirmary. This, too, has come about since the publication of *Caldey*. The Community's own doctor, Fr Senan, had for a long time been suggesting such a building and, when Fr Robert was elected Abbot, one of the first things he did was to start planning. Jackie Poole, the handyman, was on the island at the time with his son, Peter, and in a position to tackle the job.

The infirmary has been built in the corner of the monastic enclosure, and the significance of its position is that it is accessible both from the cloisters and from the guests' quarters. This means that any ladies on the island who are helping with the nursing can come into the infirmary without any question of having to violate the rule of women not being allowed in the enclosure. It was a great benefit in the nursing of Fr Anselm at the end yet, sadly, Fr Senan saw little or nothing of it. He had a stroke on Christmas Day, 1984, and died the following year on October 27th. I remember the date because it also happens to be my birthday.

Fr Anselm and Fr Senan had one thing in common. They both came late to monastic life.

Fr Senan (John) O'Connell, was in his seventy-ninth year when he died. Educated at Roscrea, he went on to Dublin University to study medicine. He became extremely well-qualified and highly regarded as a doctor and subsequently became a Colonel in the Royal Army Medical Corps. Then, in 1954, he decided to seek the monastic life and, in 1956, at the age of forty-nine, he made his profession as a Cistercian. Five years later he was ordained to the priesthood. He, again, was a man with a marvellous sense of humour and a great concern for others. The last months of his life were spent at Sancta Maria in Swansea, and I was able to call on him there a few times when I went up to the cricket. He was always keen to know how things were going with the Community, and always his parting words were to tell them they were in his prayers.

Fr Anselm (Francis) Simpson, who had celebrated his eightieth birthday the year before he died, was ordained as a priest in 1929 and awarded a Doctorate in Canon Law, *summa cum laude*, by the Angelicum, Rome, in 1932. He was for many years a Redemptorist, and then, following service during the war as an army chaplain, he transferred to the Cistercians and was professed in 1966 at the age of sixty two.

For some weeks before he died somebody had been with him all the time and, whilst the monks were at Office, I sometimes took my turn so that whichever brother would otherwise have had to stay with him could join the rest at prayer. I sat with him for an hour on the day he died, and it was an uplifting experience to see the peacefulness of a good Christian, who had given of his best according to his own lights, and was ready for whatever was to come. Those who were with him when the end came, just after midnight, said there was no last minute struggle, but just a last deep breath and the whisper of a contented sigh.

His funeral service, too, was a joyful and moving experience with the happy atmosphere he would have wished. The Abbot, in a typically brief and simple homily, reminded us how Fr Anselm had come late to the monastic life, and how he had made them all very much aware that it was their home, keeping the fire going and, at Christmas, making sure that every little bit of holly was placed just so. And he concluded by saying he felt sure that Fr Anselm would feel so at home in Heaven that he would have to make sure that the little sprig of holly was in place, just so.

Following Fr Anselm's death, his place at the refectory table was cleared and a crucifix placed by his name-plate. In the old days, when beggars used to come to the monasteries to be fed, a meal also would have been put on the table and given to the first beggar to come to the door. This no longer happens, but the custom remains of placing the crucifix. It reminds the Community that the departed is still with them in spirit and, because of what happened at Calvary, we know there is no death.

In the light of all that I have just been writing, my attitude to one particular questioner will, I hope, be better understood. It was in the days following Fr Anselm's death and, in the refectory, I had been explaining the significance of the crucifix as I have just been explaining it here. Then, in the enclosure afterwards, a rather brash young man asked, in a rather cynical and sneering tone, 'And what do these men believe will happen to them when they die?'

Now when we say we believe something we admit to an element of doubt. There were about a hundred people there and I had an end to keep up. So I weighed my words carefully and said, 'They don't believe anything. They know. They're going to Heaven. And I'll tell you something else. When I've earned the right I'm going there, too.'

'Oh indeed' he said, 'and what makes you think you'll have any right to go there?'

'Because of a promise given.'

'Oh, yes, and what promise is that?'

''In My Father's house are many mansions. If it were not so, I would have told you. I go to prepare a place for you . . . that where I am, there ye may be also.' And,' I added 'that's good enough for me. Any more questions please?'

There are those who will not agree with me, but I am prepared to argue the point.

It was at an afternoon session and, on my way down to the jetty, I called at the tea-rooms to find my chauffeur for the day and to report to Fr Stephen. I recounted as faithfully as I could what had happened. He smiled in his quiet, phlegmatic way and said, 'That's quite right. Don't argue with them. Just lay it on the line.'

Although I have known the monks for many years I grew much closer to them over those months. I had my dinner with them every day and went to at least one Office a day with them. There is no talking at meals, but it was edifying beyond words to be aware of all the nuances of the sly smile and the discreet and knowing glance.

There were a hundred and one ways in which I was made to feel part of the Community and there were so many personal jokes we shared between us.

There is a lift, too slow-moving for most of the Community to bother with it. But Fr Desiré does, because he has had a slight stroke. And I was glad of it, too, because of my arthritis. The only trouble was that, because he was the only one who normally used it, Desiré more often that not would forget to close the door, so that it would be useless to anyone wanting to summon it to another floor. Eventually I got the message through to him. Occasionally he would forget and as he came quietly in to Office, I would tap my forehead to exhort him to remember, and he would smilingly beat his breast, *mea culpa.*

On one auspicious occasion I caught Fr Bernard out in some sort of sin. Whether grievious, mortal or culpable I wouldn't know. I am not well up in these things. He was ten seconds late ringing the bell to summon the Community for Sext. Since it was his first transgression in doing the job seven times a day for more than twenty-five years the penance could not have been too horrific. Or so he tried to persuade me in an off-stage whisper. I told him it was wishful thinking on his part.

And now, before these words see the light of day, he will know the answer for himself, for, following close on the death of Peter Cummins, Fr Bernard collapsed one morning and died the same evening. He was just two months older than I was and we shared many a joke together as well as many a serious talk. Now, someone else will have to act as parish priest, someone else will have to keep an eye on the clock to ring the bell, It will all throw that extra little burden here and there on a dwindling community, and I shall miss him personally.

Above all, I was able to see something of the Cistercian spirituality. Far more than I had ever done before. With the rigours of their way of life I began to realise what support to each other they could be and how important Community was to them. I saw something of their human weaknesses and failings, of the petty irritations and how their life of prayer enabled them to react and rise above such things. All this and so much more, which I am not able to put into words. And, even more than before, I realised what a debt of gratitude the world owes to such people.

When my own time comes I would like to think I could meet it half as peacefully as Fr Anselm.

And I shall often wonder whether, in his whimsical way, he was making one of his little jokes by trying to tell me that he was working out a plan to cross to the other side at 'tuppence per person per trip.'

One day I shall know for sure. Because of that promise.

Farewell

Looking back, I suppose I might ask myself how I came to write this book. For that matter I might even ask myself how I came to be a writer.

Although, for reasons which are not relevant here, I had begun, back in 1954, to scribble odd pieces for the local paper, which eventually led me into journalism, I had neither the ambition nor intention to write a book. Then came *Cliffs of Freedom*. I wrote it purely to tell the story of my friend, Reuben Codd, a great countryman, who had forgotten more about the creatures of the wild than some so-called naturalists will ever know.

The Nature Conservancy had been persuaded by the West Wales Field Society, as constituted at that time, to acquire Skomer for the nation. The statements issued to the press about 'a place where seals and sea-birds could live in peace for ever' were enough to make people vomit when they knew of the barbarity of this same outfit's seal-ringing and bird-ringing activities. So the book had to be written. It was much criticised in some quarters by people for whose opinions I had no regard, but it is some small cause for satisfaction that it went to four editions and is still being asked for a quarter of a century later.

As far as I was concerned that was the end of the book writing but, as a result, I was asked to write a book for the schools about farming. Then I was asked to write a book about the Pembrokeshire islands, and the result was *The Sounds Between*. After that the writing, like Topsy, 'just growed.'

I had for many years known, and had dealings with, the monks of Caldey, another of Pembrokeshire's islands, and the idea was eventually put to me that I should tell their story. The result, in that case, was *Total Community*. No sooner had that appeared than various people began to say they had enjoyed it all right, but were disappointed that I had not written more about those who had lived and worked on Caldey over the years, and why didn't I write a book about Caldey more on the lines of *The Sounds*

Between. The prospect was daunting, for I knew the research involved would represent a monumental task. However, I tackled it eventually, and *Caldey* was published in the spring of 1984.

Over the years many little items have come to light to add to that which I have already written. And, of course, on the other islands of Ramsey, in particular, and Skomer and Skokholm, other things have happened which meant that the story needed bringing up-to-date. Not least satisfactory is the way in which the West Wales Naturalist Trust of Conservation under its new constitution and completely new control are coping with the task of trying to warden Skomer and Skokholm. It is not easy for them. They need the people's money to pay the warden and they need the warden to control the people. When will somebody come up with a decent thesis on the burning question as to which came first, the chicken or the egg? Still they do their best and no more can be asked than that. And it would be sad indeed if posterity were to judge the twentieth century entirely by what was happening when it was imperative for *Cliffs of Freedom* to be written. Not all the birdy people and conservationists of today are as bad as that.

I referred in these pages, when writing of Caldey, to my arthritis. I know, and accept with a good grace in the knowledge of many years of happy visiting, that I am unlikely ever again to be able to clamber about on Grassholm, and the walk from North Haven to the farm-house on Skomer would be beyond me. True, I spent a few nights on Ramsey last year and live in hopes of more. But wandering that lovely island is no longer possible and, even though Caldey is available with limitations, there will be no more collecting gulls' eggs even there. So, in many ways, I know it is bound to be farewell to the islands as far as I am concerned. But they have provided me with so many happy hours, I have my memories and I am content.

On the other hand, and this is another interpolation as the book goes to press, I have recently had a total hip replacement. The result has been so spectacular that I can hardly wait to go back and have the other hip done so maybe an Island Postscript could still be a possibility.

I would imagine, however, that it must be farewell as far as the writing on the islands is concerned. I can hardly think there will be occasion for me to write another book on them, so that this must be my last word. It will be up to others to add to them on points of fact, as and when they come to light, and to point out any mistakes.

I hope that not so many will be found and that what is left may be of some use and some interest to those who follow. Above all, as a native of what to us will always be Pembrokeshire, I hope, as I have always hoped in all my writing, that it will give some pleasure to 'my own folks.'

INDEX

Index   *175*